ClearRevise®

OCR
Creative iMedia

Illustrated revision and practice

Levels 1/2
J834 (R093, R094)

Covering:
R093: Creative iMedia in the media industry
R094: Visual identity and digital graphics

Published by
PG Online Limited
The Old Coach House
35 Main Road
Tolpuddle
Dorset
DT2 7EW
United Kingdom

sales@pgonline.co.uk
www.clearrevise.com
www.pgonline.co.uk
2022

PG ONLINE

PREFACE

Absolute clarity! That's the aim.

This is everything you need to ace your exam and beam with pride. Each topic is laid out in a beautifully illustrated format that is clear, approachable and as concise and simple as possible.

We have included worked examination-style questions with answers. This helps you understand where marks are coming from and to see the theory at work for yourself in an examination situation. There is also a set of exam-style questions at the end of each section for you to practise writing answers. You can check your answers against those given at the end of the book.

LEVELS OF LEARNING

Based on the degree to which you are able to truly understand a new topic, we recommend that you work in stages. Start by reading a short explanation of something, then try and recall what you've just read. This has limited effect if you stop there but it aids the next stage. Question everything. Write down your own summary and then complete and mark a related exam-style question. Cover up the answers if necessary but learn from them once you've seen them. Lastly, teach someone else. Explain the topic in a way that they can understand. Have a go at the different practice questions – they offer an insight into how and where marks are awarded.

ACKNOWLEDGEMENTS

Every effort has been made to trace and acknowledge ownership of copyright. The publishers will be happy to make any future amendments with copyright owners that it has not been possible to contact. The publisher would like to thank the following companies and individuals who granted permission for the use of their images or material in this textbook.

Design and artwork: Jessica Webb, Mike Bloys / PG Online Ltd
Graphics / images: © Shutterstock
Radio studio © Sunshine Seeds / Shutterstock.com   Pokémon Go screenshot © KeongDaGreat / Shutterstock.com
Stopmotion Bots © Iryna Imago / Shutterstock.com   Film set © dmitro2009 / Shutterstock.com
Rehearsal © Christian Bertrand / Shutterstock.com   Creative Commons icon © Creative Commons
Filming through window © Raketir / Shutterstock.com   Screenshots and software icons © Adobe

First edition 2022. 10 9 8 7 6 5 4 3 2 1
A catalogue entry for this book is available from the British Library
ISBN: 978-1-910523-27-8
Contributor: Jenny Gainsford
Editor: James Franklin
Consultants: Leonora Sheppard, Mike Bloys
Copyright © PG Online 2022
All rights reserved

Printed on FSC certified paper by Bell and Bain Ltd, Glasgow, UK.

FSC
www.fsc.org
MIX
Paper from responsible sources
FSC® C007785

THE SCIENCE OF REVISION

Illustrations and words

Research has shown that revising with words and pictures doubles the quality of responses by students.[1] This is known as 'dual-coding' because it provides two ways of fetching the information from our brain. The improvement in responses is particularly apparent in students when they are asked to apply their knowledge to different problems. Recall, application and judgement are all specifically and carefully assessed in public examination questions.

Retrieval of information

Retrieval practice encourages students to come up with answers to questions.[2] The closer the question is to one you might see in a real examination, the better. Also, the closer the environment in which a student revises is to the 'examination environment', the better. Students who had a test 2-7 days away did 30% better using retrieval practice than students who simply read, or repeatedly reread material. Students who were expected to teach the content to someone else after their revision period did better still.[3] What was found to be most interesting in other studies is that students using retrieval methods and testing for revision were also more resilient to the introduction of stress.[4]

Ebbinghaus' forgetting curve and spaced learning

Ebbinghaus' 140-year-old study examined the rate at which we forget things over time. The findings still hold true. However, the act of forgetting facts and techniques and relearning them is what cements them into the brain.[5] Spacing out revision is more effective than cramming – we know that, but students should also know that the space between revisiting material should vary depending on how far away the examination is. A cyclical approach is required. An examination 12 months away necessitates revisiting covered material about once a month. A test in 30 days should have topics revisited every 3 days – intervals of roughly a tenth of the time available.[6]

Summary

Students: the more tests and past questions you do, in an environment as close to examination conditions as possible, the better you are likely to perform on the day. If you prefer to listen to music while you revise, tunes without lyrics will be far less detrimental to your memory and retention. Silence is most effective.[5] If you choose to study with friends, choose carefully – effort is contagious.[7]

1. Mayer, R. E., & Anderson, R. B. (1991). Animations need narrations: An experimental test of dual-coding hypothesis. *Journal of Education Psychology*, (83)4, 484–490.

2. Roediger III, H. L., & Karpicke, J.D. (2006). Test-enhanced learning: Taking memory tests improves long-term retention. *Psychological Science*, 17(3), 249–255.

3. Nestojko, J., Bui, D., Kornell, N. & Bjork, E. (2014). Expecting to teach enhances learning and organisation of knowledge in free recall of text passages. *Memory and Cognition*, 42(7), 1038–1048.

4. Smith, A. M., Floerke, V. A., & Thomas, A. K. (2016) Retrieval practice protects memory against acute stress. *Science*, 354(6315), 1046–1048.

5. Perham, N., & Currie, H. (2014). Does listening to preferred music improve comprehension performance? *Applied Cognitive Psychology*, 28(2), 279–284.

6. Cepeda, N. J., Vul, E., Rohrer, D., Wixted, J. T. & Pashler, H. (2008). Spacing effects in learning a temporal ridgeline of optimal retention. *Psychological Science*, 19(11), 1095–1102.

7. Busch, B. & Watson, E. (2019), *The Science of Learning*, 1st ed. Routledge.

CONTENTS

Section 4   Distribution considerations

Unit R094 Visual identity and digital graphics   NEA
Topic 1   Develop visual identity

Topic 2   Plan digital graphics for products

Topic 3 Create a visual identity and digital graphics

MARK ALLOCATIONS

Green mark allocations[1] on answers to in-text questions through this guide help to indicate where marks are gained within the answers. A bracketed '1' e.g. [1] = one valid point worthy of a mark. There are often many more points to make than there are marks available so you have more opportunity to max out your answers than you may think.

TOPICS FOR THE EXAM

R093 Creative iMedia in the media industry

Information about the exam paper

Written exam: 1 hour and 30 minutes
70 marks
Section A: 10 marks
Section B: 60 marks
40% of the qualification

Specification coverage
Theoretical knowledge of creative iMedia in the media industry,
topic areas 1–4.

Topic Area 1: The media industry
Topic Area 2: Factors influencing product design
Topic Area 3: Pre-production planning
Topic Area 4: Distribution considerations

Questions
Section A: Between 7 and 10 closed response, multiple choice and
short answer questions to assess knowledge and understanding.

Section B: Context-based questions based on a short scenario.
Closed response, short answer questions and three extended
response questions. Content will be from all topic areas with at least
one question relating to each area.

CREATIVE iMEDIA IN THE MEDIA INDUSTRY

Everywhere we go, we are surrounded by media. Whether it is an advertisement on a billboard that you pass on the way to school, a computer game, a leaflet that drops through the door or the latest blockbuster film. It all forms part of the media industry.

The UK games industry has grown to be worth more than £5 billion a year employing over 20,000 people. Meanwhile, the UK film industry has maintained sales of over £3 billion a year for the last 20 years. Such industries are vast, encompassing creative media positions from directors to graphic designers, animators to sound engineers.

It's not all film and games though, the UK has an advertising industry that is three times the size of the film and games industries combined. Meanwhile, the UK publishing industry is larger than both the film industry and the games industry. Whether they be photographers, designers or typesetters, everyone involved in the industry requires a keen sense of media products and how they are creatively made to entice, persuade or entertain the end user.

The topics required for the examination enable you to understand how media products are planned along with the techniques that are used to convey meaning, create impact and engage audiences.

The topics cover the media industry, the factors influencing product design, pre-production planning and distribution considerations.

There is a lot to learn and revise in this section. Whilst the exam itself is only worth 40%, be aware that lots of what you learn in this section will help you when undertaking the non-examined assessment (NEA) units in class.

MEDIA INDUSTRY SECTORS

The media industry can be divided into two broad **sectors**, **traditional media** and **new media**.

Traditional media

Traditional media includes **film**, **television**, **radio** and **print publishing** such as posters, billboards, magazines and newspapers. It refers to industries that existed before computers and the Internet.

New media

New media is any method of communication which makes use of digital technologies for publication and distribution. It reflects the growth of technology in the media industry and includes **computer games**, **interactive media**, websites delivered via the **Internet** and **digital publishing**. This type of media is usually accessed via the Internet through computers, portable devices and Internet enabled televisions.

Interactive media covers any type of media that the user is able to interact with. Examples include a website that allows a user to find information and photos about a product, an animated advert asking the user to click to find out more, or an augmented reality smartphone game which enables users to find virtual monsters lurking in the real world.

1. A television broadcaster currently makes use of television and print publishing to advertise new upcoming programs. Identify **two** new media sectors that they could use for advertising. [2]

2. A magazine publisher creates magazines using traditional media. State **one** sector within traditional media that the magazine publisher is part of. [1]

1. *Interactive media[1] (such as a mini game on a website that engages the audience with the new TV programme), the Internet[1] (such as by creating a website to generate interest in the television programme), digital publishing[1] (such as a web banner advert).*

2. *Print publishing.[1]*

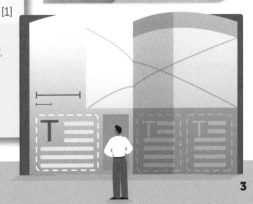

MEDIA INDUSTRY PRODUCTS

There are a wide range of media **products** that are produced by and used in different sectors.

Video

Video includes any product that makes use of moving images. It is used on traditional TV broadcasts and increasingly online with streaming services such as Netflix® and YouTube®.

Animation

Animation is a series of still images that are combined together one after the other to create an illusion of movement. Animation includes **stop-motion animation**.

Music

Music includes artist albums and singles sold on CDs, streamed, or broadcast on radio. It also includes soundtracks that add emotion to video and film.

Audio

Audio is used for voice overs in advertisements and podcasts. An important part of a video or film is the sound effects such as a window breaking or tyres screeching. Audio is used to enhance interactive media, such as a button click or 'ping' sound on a smartphone.

Print

Print products are paper-based products produced by printers. They include physical books, newspapers, magazines, leaflets, posters and brochures.

eBooks

eBooks or electronic books are non-editable digital books that are viewed using an eReader or an app on a smartphone, tablet or web browser. eReaders usually only display grayscale (black and white) and have limited layout capabilities. They are best suited to novels.

1. Explain **one** way in which a local café is able to make use of social media platforms to advertise a new offer on their range of cakes. [2]
2. Explain the purpose of **two** media products that may be contained inside an auction app. [4]

1. *A digital graphic could show the tempting range of new cakes.[1] The local cafe could use this image for targetted advertising (such as to the local area) on social media.[1]*
2. *Digital graphics (photos)[1] could show the products that are being auctioned.[1] A sound effect (such as a bell)[1] could notify the user that an auction is about to end.[1]*

Special effects

SFX includes any effects that happen live on set when filming. Examples include pyrotechnics, explosions and artificial rain. Other examples include gory wounds and prosthetics (pretend limbs) used in a film.

Visual effects

VFX are created in post-production using computers. VFX are used to create footage that is too dangerous, expensive, or difficult to create in real life, like a spaceship flying at light speed. Green screens are heavily used when creating VFX. Actors may wear body suits for motion capture with their movements then being mapped onto **computer generated (CG) characters**.

Augmented reality

Augmented Reality (AR) superimposes images and information onto a live view from a smartphone or tablet. It is used in gaming as well as modelling prototypes, such as in architecture, and visualising products in their environment.

Virtual reality

Virtual Reality (VR) uses a headset to show the user a full 360° game or video. The image will alter as the user moves their head. This allows the user to turn behind them in a 3D game. VR is also used in medical training, allowing doctors to practice without any risk or in architecture to give an immersive experience before construction begins on a building.

Other media products

Digital imaging and **graphics** are images that are created using computers, tablets or digital cameras. They include digital photography, logos and graphic design.

Digital games cover a wide range of products from online games to console games. They are mostly designed to entertain.

Websites combine digital graphics, audio and video with interactive features such as buttons and hyperlinks.

Comics and **graphic novels** are both forms of image-based storytelling. Comics tend to contain several shorter stories. Graphic novels are entire stories told in comic form with speech bubbles for spoken text.

Multimedia products are those that include a range of media such as images, text, videos, animation, sounds and buttons.
They enable the user to interact with several media technologies such as self-service checkout screens and information kiosks.

MEDIA PRODUCTS ACROSS DIFFERENT SECTORS

Media products are used to inform, influence and entertain. They are used across lots of different sectors of society or types of business as a method of communication.

Media case study

Herringbone Estate Agents sell houses in the country. Look at the following examples of how they make use of various media products across different sectors of the media industry.

Website House photos and plans

Sector	
New media – Digital publishing via the Internet	
Product	
Digital imaging / digital photos	
Purpose	 
To inform prospective house buyers and entice them into viewing a property.	

Billboard posters

Sector	**Purpose**	
Traditional media – Print publishing	To advertise and promote a new property development. This will generate awareness and interest in the project.	
Product		
Digital imaging and graphics		

Leaflets

Sector

Traditional media –
Print publishing

Product

Digital imaging
and graphics

Purpose

A leaflet can also advertise
and promote a property
development. It works differently
to a billboard as people have
longer to read it. Therefore, it
may contain further information
such as services offered, an
email address and the location
of the estate agent's offices.

1. Herringbone Estate Agents has branches across the UK. They already
   have a radio advert and print advert to promote the brand.

   Identify **one** other sector of traditional media that they could use
   to advertise. [1]

2. Herringbone Estate Agents already make use of traditional media print
   products, such as billboard posters and leaflets to advertise their brand
   and services.

   Describe how Herringbone Estate Agents could make use of **two** new
   media sectors such as the Internet and digital publishing to inform
   potential customers of new houses that have come onto the market. [4]

3. Explain why Herringbone Estate Agents decides to use a number of
   media sectors to advertise rather than just one. [3]

1. *Television[1], cinema advertising (before the film starts).[1]*

2. *Herringbone Estate Agents could take the layout and style of the
   billboard poster and use it as a template for a banner advert[1] which
   they put onto social media networks that are used by prospective
   homebuyers or those that live nearby.[1]*

   *They could take the graphics, layout and content of the leaflet and
   turn it into a short online catalogue/e-book[1] that customers could
   either download or make use of in a website that allows them to
   turn the pages of the book by pressing an arrow button.[1]*

3. *This enables different target audiences to be reached[1], for
   example, a daytime television advert may appeal to people that
   don't go to work[1] whilst leaflets through the letterbox of local
   houses would appeal to those who live locally.[1]*

   *Different media sectors have different advantages. For instance, a
   radio advert will play to a captive audience[1], so lots of people will
   repeatedly hear about the brand.[1] By contrast, sending a full colour
   brochure to interested customers[1] allows them to fully appreciate
   the best features of a property and imagine living there.[1]*

JOB ROLES IN THE MEDIA INDUSTRY

There are a variety of job roles within the media industry. In smaller scale media projects, one person may perform more than one of these roles. In larger projects, job roles may be divided up into even more specialist positions. Some job roles in the media industry are specific to one of the pre-production, production or post-production phases of a project. Other roles work across multiple phases of a project.

Key phases in a media product

Pre-production → **Production** → **Post-production**

This phase plans the execution of every step of production to ensure the most effective use of crew, time and resources. In a film, for example, this would be where you finalise the script and hire the production crew.

This is when the media product is created. If making a film or television show, this would include the actual filming of the actors or scenes.

For a magazine, this stage would involve producing the photographs, graphics and copywriting.

This is the final phase where the media product is prepared for launch. The tasks here are varied and depend on the media product. In film or television it could include: editing video footage; editing the sound and adding sound effects; adding special effects; adding titles and graphics.

Technical roles

Camera operator

A **camera operator** films what is happening, whether for a TV documentary, feature film or an advert during the **production** phase. They must consider the framing, movement and composition of each shot and select the appropriate camera equipment to use under the instruction of the **director**.

Games programmer/developer

A **games developer** writes the code for games on devices such as PCs, consoles and smartphones. They will make use of 3D models and audio assets created by graphic designers and composers. They will work closely with scriptwriters to create an engaging experience for players.

Sound editor

In film and TV production, sound and video are recorded separately during production and need to be combined in post-production. A **sound editor** is a highly skilled job and is responsible for creating, enhancing and mixing any music, sound effects and dialogue and synchronising these with the pictures.

Audio technician

An **audio technician** is involved in setting up, operating and maintaining audio recording equipment such as microphones and mixers. The role might include recording on set during production or the editing and mixing of sounds in post-production.

Video editor

A **video editor** is a key role in post-production. They are responsible for editing footage such as video, special effects, visual effects and graphics. The video editor will work closely with the director to complete final products such as films, commercials, television programmes and music videos.

Web developer

Front-end developers

A **front-end developer** creates and maintains websites using one or more programming languages such as HTML or JavaScript. They will work with graphic designers and photographers who make the digital assets for the site.

Back-end developers

Back-end developers are responsible for the programming that makes a site work, such as that needed to process credit card orders or update stock in a database.

1. When producing a film, a director will be involved in the pre-production, production and post-production phases. State the most likely phase that a camera operator will be required for. [1]

2. Explain why a sound editor and video editor may need to work together during the production of a film. [2]

1. The production phase.[1]

2. During the pre-production phase[1] the video editor and sound editor will work with the director to determine the soundtrack and sound effects that will be required to match each scene.[1] If the video editor makes changes to scenes during post-production[1] they will need to keep the sound editor informed as this may affect the background music required.[1]

CREATIVE ROLES IN THE MEDIA INDUSTRY

Graphic designer

A **graphic designer** creates visuals for a variety of media products such as magazines, brochures and websites. As part of both the **pre-production** and **production phases**, a graphic designer will work to a brief, producing rough sketches and designs to share with a client. They will create suitable images and graphics that might include hand drawn designs, photos and illustrations using a range of specialist software.

Content creator

A **content creator** generally creates content for websites, blog posts and social media. They may create simple digital media assets including text, video and audio for a specific audience. The aim is often to generate awareness of a brand or to advertise a product or service.

Copy writer

A **copy writer** creates the text or **copy** for advertising or marketing purposes, usually to persuade a person or group of people that a product or service is just what they need.

A copy writer could write the content for print adverts, radio advertisements, product descriptions or social media posts.

Animator

An **animator** usually works during the production phase of a project. More traditionally, animation involves creating a series of still images that can be combined together to create the illusion of movement. Alternatively, in stop-motion animation, clay models are moved slightly before each new frame is taken.

The majority of animation is made in 3D. Here, computer animators and modellers use storyboards and a brief from the director to create 3D computer models that are animated using specialist software.

Photographer

A **photographer** captures high quality, impactful images to help communicate a message or story. This may be for fashion and beauty, lifestyle or advertising. They work closely with the client to produce the right visual content appropriate for the end use such as a billboard, magazine or website. They may be involved in the editing and post-production phase too. Photographers may also sell their work to **image libraries** where other designers buy the work as assets for their own projects.

Scriptwriter

A **scriptwriter** writes and develops scripts for film, TV, radio and computer games. They might adapt an existing work such as a book or create an original work. Script writers create characters, dialogue and the plot as well as providing details about the setting and location.

Web designer

A **web designer** designs, plans and creates websites. They may create new websites or edit existing ones. A web designer uses their creative skills to combine images, sounds, videos and text together to meet client requirements.

User experience (UX) designers will focus on the experience of the end user and make sure the site is as easy to use as possible.

Illustrator / graphic artist

An **illustrator** creates the drawings or images for a wide range of media products such as children's books, magazines and greetings cards. An illustrator may use hand drawings, graphics tablets or tablets with a stylus pen.

Graphic artists will produce layouts for books, brochures, magazines and posters choosing how copy, images and illustration will work together on the page.

1. Identify **one** creative job role other than web designer that might contribute to the creation of a new website. [2]
2. Describe **two** tasks that might be the responsibility of a content creator. [4]

> 1. *A photographer[1] would take photographs / produce image content to appear on the web pages[1], a graphic designer[1] could create graphics such as a logo for the website[1], a copy writer[1] could write the text content for the web pages.[1]*
>
> 2. *Writing blog posts[1] about a new product[1], creating social media posts[1] to promote an event[1], writing text for company website[1] with information about the company[1], generating website traffic[1] by writing engaging content[1], increasing sales / brand awareness[1] by writing about products.[1]*

SENIOR JOB ROLES IN THE MEDIA INDUSTRY

Senior job roles

Campaign manager

Companies need to sell products, e.g. a film, a new toy or a service such as a restaurant. A marketing campaign will be created to drive awareness within the target audience. Such campaigns may use many different media products and sectors. A **campaign manager** is responsible for planning and managing marketing campaigns. For instance, the marketing campaign for a film may involve coordinating the release of trailers, billboards, bus advertising, television teasers and interviews for television programs.

Editor

An **editor** controls the content of print publications such as books, magazines, newspapers and websites. They plan, organise and review materials to check it is suitable for the publication and the target audience. An editor may make changes to the tone and structure of copy or alter titles or images to maximise the impact of a message.

Creative director

A **creative director** leads a team of graphic designers, illustrators, copy writers, photographers and other creatives. They are the 'ideas' people who help to shape the creative direction of a project and help the client deliver their marketing strategy. They ensure production and client requirements are met.

Director

A **director** oversees the creative direction of a production such as a TV programme or film. They work with storyboard artists, actors and crew in production and other creatives such as video editors in post-production to shape the style of the production. A director may take years to go from a script to the end product of a film.

Production manager

A **production manager** is responsible for liaising with different departments. They will have a key role in the pre-production phase of a project and may be responsible for scheduling and budgets. This is a role that requires substantial industry experience, a detailed understanding of the production process and the ability to accurately organise multiple people and resources.

1. Explain **one** way a creative director contributes to the creation of an advertising campaign. [2]
2. Describe **two** ways that a director contributes to the creation of a film. [4]

1. *A creative director leads the creative team[1] developing the direction of the campaign,[1] pitching ideas to the client[1] and checking the campaign meets the client requirements.[1]*
2. *Film directors are the creative lead[1] whose vision, look and style for the film will need to be met.[1] In pre-production, the director works with a script or screenwriter[1] and appoints the director of photography and casting director.[1] They work with a storyboard artist[1] to plan the production.[1] During production, they work closely with camera crew[1] to capture the best shots.[1] They also work closely with actors[1] to bring out their best performance.[1] In post-production, they lead the editing process[1] which is reviewed by producers before being signed off for release.[1]*

EXAMINATION PRACTICE

FastFit has just opened a new sports centre and they want to attract customers in the local area. Their facilities include a 25-metre pool, fully equipped gym, and a range of exercise classes. FastFit want to create a marketing campaign that will appeal to people aged 16-40 who are interested in being fit and staying healthy.

You are the campaign manager in charge of attracting customers to the gym.

(a) FastFit don't want any video to be produced for their marketing campaign.

Identify **two** appropriate sectors within traditional and new media that could be used in the marketing campaign. [2]

(b) Identify **three** appropriate products, other than a **video**, **TV advert** and **website**, that could be used to promote the new local sports centre to local residents. [3]

FastFit have been persuaded that a 30 second video should be created for use in their website. The video will include footage of people using the gym equipment, attending classes and using the swimming pool.

(c) Compare and contrast the role of a campaign manager with that of a camera operator in the production of the video. [4]

(d) Other than **camera operator** and **video editor**, identify **two** other job roles that are likely to be needed to create the video. [2]

(e) Three phases are required when creating a **video** or **film**. What is the first phase that occurs before the **camera operator** is able to record any footage? [1]

Tick (✓) the correct box.
A. ☐ Planning
B. ☐ Post-production
C. ☐ Pre-production
D. ☐ Production

(f) A **video editor** will be involved in the **post-production** of the video.
Describe the main responsibilities of a video editor in producing the video. [3]

(g) Once the video is complete, identify the job roles of **two** other people that the campaign manager is likely to work with to create the website that the video will be part of. [3]·

(h) Outline **two** ways a content creator might use the 30 second video to raise awareness of the new sports centre. [4]

(i) FastFit has given a budget for the marketing campaign. This is controlled by the campaign manager. Identify the job role which will be responsible for making sure that the video stays within budget. [1]

PURPOSE OF MEDIA PRODUCTS

A media product usually has a **purpose** or a reason for its development. Some media products will have more than one purpose. The purpose is closely linked to the type of media product. The purpose of a billboard, for example, is usually to advertise or promote a product or service. By contrast, the purpose of a TV programme may be to entertain.

Examples

The main purposes of media products are to:

Advertise / promote

There are a wide range of media products with this purpose including print **adverts** such as billboards, posters and leaflets, TV/radio advertising as well as online banner advertising on websites and social media.

Entertain

Most people spend a large amount of time each day being **entertained** by media products including TV shows, films, radio broadcasts, books, apps and computer games. Remember, many broadcasters need to make their content as compelling as possible as they make their money from advertising between programs.

Educate

Many media products aim to **educate**. Textbooks combine text, images and photos and are suited to independent study and revision. eLearning products are able to add interaction and video to the learning experience. Apps and games are able to teach through play.

Inform

Posters are often used to display information such as your location on a map in a theme park. Information leaflets on health or financial products also help to **inform**.

Influence

Media products often aim to **influence** behaviour. This may be used as part of advertising. It may also be used by governments or schools to promote healthy or safe behaviours.

---

1. Identify **one** print publishing product that might be used to promote a new film. [1]

2. A bus company has commissioned a set of posters to reduce the amount of chewing gum being left on their buses. Explain **one** way in which this purpose could be achieved. [2]

1. *Poster,[1] magazine advert,[1] billboard.[1]*

2. *The poster could promote passengers[1] to make use of bins provided.[1] The poster could inform passengers[1] of the cost of removing chewing gum.[1] A photo showing disgust at chewing gum stuck to clothes[1] could influence passengers to consider their actions.[1]*

USE OF COLOUR IN MEDIA PRODUCTS

Colour choices

The content, style and layout will all be adapted to meet the particular purpose of a media product.

Colour choices may be used to create a mood or feeling from a media product. They might also be used to make certain objects stand out or draw attention to a particular element.

Warm colours

Warm shades are associated with the sun, fire and heat. They work well in creating a warm and inviting feel. Reds may be used to attract the eye to key messages.

Cool colours

These are associated with water and ice, and can be calming and peaceful. Shades of green are often used for products that are environmental, natural or related to money.

Creating mood

Different combinations of colours are also used to create a mood within a graphic product.

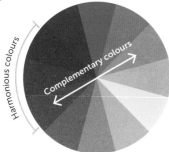

Harmonious colours

Harmonious colours, also known as **analogous colours**, are found next to each other on the colour wheel, for example purple, purple-blue and blue. Together, these colours create a feeling of calm.

Complementary colours

Complementary colours, also known as **opposite colours**, are found directly opposite each other on the colour wheel, for example blue and orange. Placing complementary colours next to each other gives a vivid, vibrant and exciting feel which adds drama to a product.

You are designing a poster promoting a summer beach holiday club for children.
Explain the colours you would use for the campaign.   [2]

A use of complementary bright colours such as orange and blue[1] would be appealing to children[1] (who would pester their parents to buy the holiday) and help to give the feeling of warm sun and sea.[1] Alternatively, harmonious colours, such as oranges and yellows,[1] would help to give a warm summery feeling.[1]

STYLE, CONTENT AND LAYOUT

Positioning of elements

Elements of media products need to be carefully **positioned** to achieve a pleasing composition. Look at the flyer for Zorange below. Zorange is a new orange juice drink that aims to be healthy and to appeal to young children and families. Notice how the orange juice drink is positioned to flow across the page, bursting with energy. This draws the eye across the page and encourages people to read the copy (text) in the lower right.

Conventions of genre

Different genres will use typical components and techniques. These are known as **conventions**. The drinks advertisements below both show the product clearly. The logo is shown in the lower right of each media product, helping the viewer to identify the product.

Adaptation to purpose

The Zorange billboard and flyer are **adapted** to meet different purposes. Billboard advertisements aim to build brand awareness of the drink. Drivers have little time to view a billboard, so very little text is used and the visual impact is key. Consumers have more time to read a flyer so more information about the product is included along with an offer to encourage them to purchase.

Visual and audio style

The **style** of a media product is built using many components such as graphics, colour, layout and tone of language. Each of these components work together to produce an overall style that becomes part of brand recognition. It is important that the style matches the purpose of the media product.

For instance, a television **advert** for a high-end sports car may use fast panning shots to indicate speed and energy whilst striking colours with a black background could help to give a futuristic feel. The roar of the engine may be prominent in a radio advert.

By contrast, a magazine advert for a spacious, practical car aims to **influence** readers by showing a happy scene of a family enjoying outdoor life which is aspirational and appealing. This allows the reader to imagine the possibilities that buying the car gives them.

The style of each type of advert will be completely different to satisfy different audiences and purposes.

Look at the flyer for Zorange. Describe how the style, content and layout have helped to promote their new drink and brand. [4]

The orange juice photo flows freely out of the glass[1] helping to suggest a fresh new drink with an energising taste.[1] The drink flows across the page[1] drawing the reader in to read the copy on the lower right.[1] The colour scheme uses bright harmonious colours from orange to yellow.[1] These not only match the colour of the fruit,[1] but also give a feeling of positivity with the invigorating colours.[1] The tone of language used in the copy is friendly and informal,[1] helping to build a connection with readers and persuade them to try the product.[1] The flyer places the logo in a conventional place on the lower right[1] which helps the reader to identify the brand.[1]

LANGUAGE AND TONE IN MEDIA PRODUCTS

Formal and informal language

The language used in media products may be formal or informal. The purpose of the product will affect the type of language used. For instance, a textbook aims to educate, so will use more formal language, whereas a comic strip, used to entertain, may use shorter sentences, slang and informal language.

Tone of language

It is important that the **tone of language** used in a media product matches the purpose of the product. A newspaper might use a serious, logical and balanced tone to give a feeling of trust. By contrast, an opinion column may make use of a critical or forceful tone to help persuade an audience towards a point of view or campaign the paper is running.

A content creator is working for a local charity for homeless people and creating a blog post for their website. The post will discuss the difficulties of living on the streets whilst hoping to encourage people to donate to the charity.

Explain **two** ways in which the content creator's use of language may help in encouraging people to donate to the charity.   [4]

The language used is likely to be formal[1] as this will help to build trust in the charity and their campaign.[1]

When quoting homeless people, informal language may be used[1] so that the language appears authentic.[1]

The tone of language will need to be thoughtful and measured[1] to show respect to the people being covered.[1] At the same time, passionate and persuasive language[1] could help to drive people to the campaign,[1] whilst hopeful and optimistic language would help people to realise the difference their donations could make.[1]

AUDIENCE DEMOGRAPHICS AND SEGMENTATION

Target audience

The **target audience** is the set of people who a media product is aimed at. For instance, a film company may have made a documentary film about a popular boy band and have identified that their target audience for the film is mostly teenage girls. The film company will consider the characteristics of the target audience, known as the demographics. They will then use this to choose which **segment** of the population the marketing campaign should be aimed at. This allows media products, such as advertising posters, to be made more appealing to the target audience.

Location

If a local cake shop is only able to deliver cakes up to 10 miles away, the target audience's location would be people who live within 10 miles of the shop. Products may have a target audience that is local, national or international.

Ethnicity

Ethnic groups are defined as a group of people who have a common culture, country, religion or language. Media products may focus on a particular **ethnicity**. It is important not to offend or alienate anyone with the content of a media product.

Interests / lifestyle

By understanding the hobbies and **interests** of an audience, media producers can identify what engages them. For instance, an outdoor adventure company has established that most of their customers enjoy horse riding. If a designer of a leaflet knows this, they may focus on the interest of horse riding more than other facilities.

Gender

Media products may be aimed more towards one **gender** than another. It is important that advertising and designs do not stereotype gender roles even if the target audience for a product is more likely to be one gender.

Occupation / Income

An **occupation** is the type of job that an audience does. When segmenting by occupation and audience, the category may be broad, for instance, middle income earners who work in an office.

Education

Audiences are often segmented by the highest level of **education** they have achieved such as GCSEs, A Levels or degrees. Some publications may specifically aim at an audience with specialist knowledge in an area.

Age

Age groups may be clearly defined, such as 18-24, or use descriptive terms such as 'teenagers' or 'retired people'.

You are designing a poster advertising a new feature film about camping and fishing. The film is aimed at 7–10 year olds. One category of audience segmentation would be by age. [2]

(a) Identify **one** other category of audience segmentation.

(b) Explain **one** way that the identified age group will affect the poster design.

(a) Interests[1] / lifestyle,[1] whether they like camping/fishing.[1]

(b) Simple language[1] will be used so that they can understand it easily.[1] Use of bright colours[1] should be considered as this will appeal to the age group.[1]

CLIENT BRIEF AND REQUIREMENTS

Before creating a media product, it is important that everyone involved understands the **client requirements** of the project. These requirements will be given in the **client brief**.

Client brief formats

The client brief is usually a **written document** that gives the key requirements of a project. Key people involved in the project, such as a campaign manager, production manager, and creative director will have **meetings** or **discussions** to develop the final client requirements. It is important that the creative team have asked sufficient questions so that they understand the **purpose** of the project they are working on. Meetings may be **formal** or **informal**. The budget for any project will often need to be **negotiated**.

Briefs may be communicated as paper documents, attachments to email or via other electronic documents. By clearly noting the project requirements of the client, the creative team will all understand the aims and expectations.

Project constraints

A client brief often contains mandatory requirements that the product must meet. These may be technical, such as a three-fold leaflet, or creative constraints, such as the need to use a bright colour scheme. Client briefs can constrain the possible options that are available in the planning and production of media products.

Remember: In an 'explain' question, you get 1 mark for making a valid point and 1 mark for explaining it.

Giving two separate points, with no explanation, will only get you 1 mark.

1. TekWatch has just created a new smart watch. They now need to create the media products for a marketing campaign for the watch. They have decided to commission an advertising company, Blaze Creative, to create their media products. The campaign manager for TekWatch will be in charge of coordinating the project and client requirements.

   (a) Identify the client in this case. [1]

   (b) Name **two** ways in which TekWatch and Blaze Creative are able to collaborate over the written brief. [2]

   (c) Explain how a client brief would inform a graphic designer in the pre-production planning stage. [2]

   (a) TekWatch[1] is the client (they are commissioning the services of Blaze).

   (b) Meetings,[1] discussions[1] via email/ video conferencing.[1]

   (c) The client requirements contained in the brief[1] will give guidance on/ constrain what can be used when generating ideas[1] during the pre-production planning.

Client requirements

The **client requirements** that are given in the brief usually contain the following:

Type of product

The product that is being **commissioned**. For example, 'print posters for bus shelters'.

Timescales

Key dates and deadlines for the project.

Audience

This will show which segment of people are being targeted – for example, boys aged 13–16.

Purpose

The key objective for the media product, such as to advertise or influence.

Client ethos

The media product will need to align with the client's values and beliefs.

Content

The components that need to be part of the media product, such as key information, images, video, sound or functionality.

Genre, style and theme

The look and feel of the product.
This may include the 'brand voice', and any emotions that the product should generate in the audience.

Actual client briefs may use different headings or terms to these, however, they are likely to include the same client requirements within them.

BlazeCreative
Client Brief

Forest Stay TV Marketing Campaign

Company background
Forest Stay is a well established holiday provider for relaxing woodland breaks, it has three UK holiday villages in rural locations. After a change in market position they now provide physical activities, such as swimming, zip wires and cycling, in a family friendly environment.

Objective
Reposition the brand from its existing position as quiet rural holiday destination to an exciting action-packed holiday for active kids and parents.

Target
Parents aged 30-50 with children aged 5-15.
Household income £40k - £100k.

Brand voice
Active / high energy.

Execution requirements
The client would like this to be scheduled for peak time evening television.

2. Forest Stay have just commissioned Blaze Creative for their next marketing campaign. The client brief is given above.
   (a) State the media product that Blaze Creative needs to make. [1]
   (b) State **two** features of the target audience required in the brief. [2]
   (c) Describe how the brief will affect the style of the television advertisement. [2]

   (a) *Television advertisements.[1]*

   (b) *Parents,[1] aged 30–50,[1] children,[1] aged 5–15[1], household income £40k - £100k.[1]*

   (c) *The brand voice is active and high energy.[1] The television will therefore need to show families doing high energy activities[1] such as water slides / BMX jumps / fast zip wires.[1]*

RESEARCH METHODS

Primary research methods

Primary research is data or research that is collected directly from customers, **surveys** or **focus groups**.

Research methods

Before a client brief is created, or during the planning phase, it is often important to research the target audience and what will appeal to them.

Research may also be carried out during the production phase.

Research data

Quantitative information

This makes use of data which can be measured numerically – think 'quantity'. For instance, if a survey showed that 63% of people preferred a colour scheme to be blue this would be **quantitative** information.

Qualitative information

This gives fuller descriptions from research – think 'quality'. For instance, an open question on the layout of a page may determine that it is cluttered, confusing and contains too much information – this is a 'quality' of the design.

Focus groups

These consist of a group of people chosen to represent the target audience to discuss and give opinions about a product.

➕ Used to share sample material with the group and hold a discussion.

➖ Only a small sample that might not be representative of the entire target audience.

Interviews

These take place with individuals or small groups of people. Researchers have conversations on a topic either face to face, online or via telephone.

➕ Used to get detailed answers to questions and can ask for clarification.

➖ Time consuming way to collect data.

Online surveys

Electronic forms are used to gather data from a large sample of individuals. There could be a mixture of open and closed questions.

➕ Large data sets may be collected quickly then automatically analysed by a computer.

➖ Participants need an Internet connection and the technical ability to be able to complete the survey.

Questionnaires

Questionnaires are paper based forms containing questions. They contain tick boxes or lines to indicate where answers are to be completed.

➕ Easily accessible to anyone without the need for technology.

➖ Paper forms can be lost, and inputting data into a computer for analysis can be time consuming.

Secondary research methods

Secondary research is the use of data and information that already exists. For instance, when making a documentary, books, archive material, recordings and footage may be used.

➕ Typically cheaper as the more costly data gathering has already been completed by someone else.

➕ May be combined with primary research methods.

➖ Not always in a suitable format or an adequate answer to specific questions.

➖ Researchers must check how trustworthy and reliable the source is.

Books and journals

➕ Publishers employ editors to check facts, so these are normally reliable sources.

➕ Academic and scientific journals will use peer review where other experts check the content.

➖ Books and journals are expensive to buy.

➖ It takes time to find the relevant information.

Websites on the Internet

➕ Quick and easy to check.

➕ Many sites are free to use.

➖ There is a wide variation of quality.

Newspapers

➕ As with books, an editor will help to ensure quality.

➖ Many articles draw on secondary research and may be interpretations of the original findings.

Television

➕ Good for obtaining quotes and video footage of events.

➖ It takes time to go through footage to find the correct clip.

1. You are carrying out audience research to understand what makes people decide to buy a new pair of trainers.
   Identify **two** primary research methods other than questionnaires. [2]

2. A researcher is working on a television documentary about penguins.
   Give **one** advantage and **one** disadvantage of using television as a secondary research source. [2]

   1. *Focus groups,[1] interviews,[1] online surveys.[1]*

   2. *Advantages: The footage found could be incorporated into the documentary.[1] Any footage of interviews with experts would probably contain reliable information.[1]*

      Disadvantages: It will take time to view lots of footage.[1] The raw data and original sources for any facts may not be available.[1] Some television programs may be biased and do not provide a neutral point of view.[1]

USING MEDIA CODES

Media codes

Media products may make use of media codes and conventions that help convey meaning, create impact and engage audiences.

Symbolic codes

Symbolic codes are not part of the media product itself, but part of our experience within society.

For example, a man kneeling down and giving a woman a ring would be a symbolic code for asking to get married.

Symbolic codes are created by acting, colour and mise-en-scène (arrangement of the set, props, costume and actors).

Technical codes

Technical codes are specific to the type of media product being created.

For example, a film could use very fast pans and cuts during a car chase. This would be a technical code to suggest speed and urgency. However, this technical code could not be used on a poster.

Technical codes are created by camera techniques, transitions, movement, lighting and audio.

Written codes

Written codes are specific to the printed language and spoken language (dialogue) used in media products.

For example, a poster for a period drama may use a traditional font and formal language to help users understand that the film is set in the past.

- Style of language
- Dialogue
- Typography

Colour

Colour helps to give media products mood and feeling.

The frame below is from a tense horror film where a woman is helping to rescue a prisoner. The background is dark black helping to suggest secrecy and suspense. The warm harmonious colours from the lamp, makeup and costume are symbolic codes that help to convey the positive act that the woman is carrying out.

Notice how a symbolic code of a finger to the mouth is also used here to suggest secrecy.

Graphics

The two **graphics** below influence, advertise and reach the audience in different ways.

Impresso uses traditional graphics for their logo with clean lines to give a sophisticated and stylish feel to their stores.

By contrast, the graphics for the iced coffee poster show cooling ice. The playful splashing of the coffee helps to give a refreshing feel on a summer's day at the beach. Notice how other features such as bright colours and a flowing font type help to enhance the impact of the poster or magazine advert..

Typography

Typography refers to the style and size of the lettering used in a design. Designers will spend a long time choosing or designing a font style that conveys a certain meaning or creates an impact. **Emphasis** is created using specific font types along with bold and italic variations.

Font types

Font types, also known as **typefaces** fall into a number of categories.

Sans serif

A **sans-serif** typeface does not contain any serifs. The French word 'sans' means 'without', so these fonts are 'without serifs'.

Sans-serif typefaces are often used with modern designs, especially where they are appealing to a more youthful audience.

Sans-serif fonts are often easier to read on smartphones and computer displays.

Serif

A **serif** typeface has small additional lines or strokes on the beginning and end of each letter. These help to create a traditional look. They are commonly used in books, newspapers and magazines as they make large quantities of text easier to read.

Decorative

Decorative typefaces allow the designer to give additional meaning or impact to words.

They are often harder to read so only used occasionally, such as for a title or logo.

Decorative
Decorative

A leaflet has been created for teenagers promoting exercise. The front of the leaflet should convey an active lifestyle and enjoyment from keeping fit. The client isn't happy with the current font style that has been chosen.

Explain **two** suitable font styles or typeface that could be used instead for the text. [2]

For the heading, a decorative typeface[1] could help in giving impact[1] and be more appropriate than a serif font style.[1]

For the other text, a sans-serif[1] typeface would help give a modern feel appropriate for teenagers.[1]

Alternative responses include different types of font with an appropriate explanation.

CAMERA TECHNIQUES

Whether planning a feature film, music video or magazine front cover image, camera angles and shots are carefully chosen to help create meaning for an audience or create impact in a scene.

Camera shots and angles

A **camera shot** refers to what is seen in the frame – what can be seen through the camera. They are useful in establishing the setting and characters in a scene. The **camera angle** refers to the position of the camera in relation to the subject or object. They are used to help the viewer understand the scene, for example, the relationships between two characters.

A scene might be filmed using multiple camera shots and angles, combined in post-production.

Close-up shot

A **close-up** shot is taken at close range to the subject. A close-up allows the viewer to see detail such as expressions or emotions. It can also highlight a pattern or detail on an object.

Extreme close-up shot

An **extreme close-up** shot focuses on a small part of the subject such as the eyes or mouth. This shot tells the viewer exactly where to look and can effectively communicate the emotional state of the subject. It can also focus on a specific part of an object, highlighting a small, but important, detail that might otherwise be missed.

Medium shot

A **medium shot**, or **mid shot**, shows an actor or group of actors from the waist up. It is used to capture conversations whilst giving some information about the setting and the body language of the subjects. It is the standard shot used for interviews or dialogue.

Long shot

A **long shot**, also known as a **wide shot**, shows the characters and objects in their surroundings. It helps immerse the audience into the film and is often used in **establishing shots**. It's also used for action scenes to give the viewer a broad view of the action.

Extreme long shot

An **extreme long shot**, or **extreme wide** gives impressive views of the location. Aerial shots may sweep across mountains or to show entire cities.

Low angle shot

A **low angle shot** is achieved by pointing the camera up from a low height at the subject or object. This has the effect of making the subject look larger and more important. It can be combined with a high angle shot to show the difference in power between two characters.

High angle shot

A **high angle shot** positions the camera higher than the subject, pointing down at them. This can make the character seem weak or vulnerable. It can also give a sense of isolation and make the viewer fearful for their fate.

Aerial shot

An **aerial shot** is taken when the camera position is high up, usually filmed from a helicopter, crane, or drone. It may show a vast expanse of landscape or a bird's eye view of a city. These shots are often used as establishing shots at the start of films to set a key location, create impact and engage audiences.

Over the shoulder shot

An **over the shoulder** shot is used during a conversation and puts the viewer in the character's shoes. It also allows the viewer to see how a character responds to the conversation and helps create intimacy between two characters. Scenes will often alternate between characters so that the viewer can see how each of them respond in the conversation.

1. You have been asked to produce a storyboard for a 30 second TV advert for a new soft drink and have included camera shots and angles. Explain why this information is useful. [2]

2. The director of a new super-hero film would like to show the audience that the character on screen is a powerful villain. Explain the camera shot or angle you would choose to show this. [2]

   1. *Camera shots and angles help give meaning / impact to the advert.[1] The director and actors will understand what emotion and meaning is trying to be given in the shot.[1] Further planning, including the hire of equipment, such as a crane, may result from understanding the shots and angles that need to be produced.[1] The camera operator and other crew will know which shot to set up before they arrive on set.[1]*

   2. *A low angle shot[1] from below the character, looking up[1] would make them look powerful and important.[1] A long shot[1] could establish them in a powerful location such as a castle or impressive sky scraper.[1]*

CAMERA MOVEMENT

Pan

Panning moves the camera left and right horizontally. This may be used to follow characters as they walk or to follow a car as it drives past.

Tilt

Tilting pivots the camera up and down vertically. This might be used to take in a scene, for example, conveying the height of skyscrapers in a city.

Zooming

The lens of a camera can be zoomed in or out to make the subject appear closer or further away. The camera itself does not move, but the focal point changes. Zooming into a subject may help to draw the viewer towards a specific detail, whilst zooming out will help to reveal the wider context of a scene.

! Note

A tripod should be used to give smooth tilting and panning.

Track and dolly

A **tracking shot** is used when the camera follows one or more subjects, immersing the viewer in the scene. The camera might be mounted on a dolly (a platform on wheels on which the camera is mounted) and placed on a track in order to achieve smooth movement.

Tracking shots can also be made with a handheld camera, for example following the subject when they are running, which results in an unsteady and jerky shot. Handheld shots can increase the intensity of a scene, creating a sense of panic or to highlight intimacy and emotion.

A television drama follows the lives of street dancers. The director wants to use camera movement to give a greater impact during a climatic dance routine.

Describe how camera movement could help the director achieve their vision. [4]

A tracking shot / track and dolly[1] could be used to track across the dance routine[1] allowing the viewer to see many different dancers.[1] A camera on a crane / aerial shot[1] could move over / around the dancers[1] allowing the whole routine to be seen at once from engaging angles.[1] Panning[1] could be used to follow the movement of a single dancer.[1]

TRANSITIONS

Transitions describe how an editor moves from one shot to another. They are added after filming, during post-production and help a story to flow.

Cut

A **cut** goes immediately from one shot to another. The term comes from when an editor would physically cut film and then add the next shot.

This can be used to good effect when moving between two characters talking or when using footage taken from multiple angles.

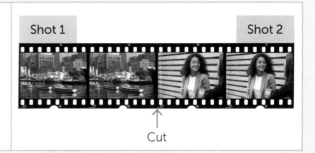

Dissolve

Dissolves are used to fade from one shot to another. This transition has the effect of showing time passing. It may also give a dream like quality to the scene.

Fade

A **fade in** or **fade out** is one of the most used transitions. The shot fades in or out from black. This is usually used at the start and end of a film. It may also be used to separate significant chapters in a film.

Wipe

A **wipe** is when one shot replaces another by moving from one side of the frame to another. It may be used to show that the story is jumping to a different plot line or location.

1. Complete the sentence: Transitions are added in during the _____ phase.
   Choose from **pre-production**, **production** or **post-production**. [1]
2. A television show is including a flash back scene to when the main character was younger.
   Explain a suitable transition that could be used. [2]

1. *Transitions are added in during the **post-production** phase.[1]*
2. *A dissolve / cross-fade[1] transition as the slower transition is able to represent the passing of time.[1] Accept other transitions with an appropriate reason for their use.*

MISE-EN-SCÈNE, LIGHTING AND AUDIO

Mise-en-scène

Mise-en-scène means the placement of actors and objects for a scene. It refers to anything that is seen through the lens of the camera including the **costumes**, **lighting**, **props**, **set design**, **location**, actor positions and movement (**blocking**) and **make-up**.

The mise-en-scène is how all these elements work together to create the mood and feeling of the final shot.

1. Identify **three** elements of the mise-en-scène that help to create the mood of a scene. [3]

   1. *Costumers,[1] lighting,[1] props,[1] set design,[1] location,[1] blocking,[1] makeup.[1]*

Lighting

The **lighting** of a shot, whether filming on location or in a studio environment is important in creating an atmosphere. It helps to convey character emotions and highlight certain props.

In a studio environment this can be carefully controlled. When filming on location, the director will have to carefully consider the time of day, **position** of the sun and weather to create the right shot. If artificial light is required, the positioning needs to appear natural.

High key lighting

High key lighting is bright with very few shadows in the frame. This style is commonly seen in musicals, classic Hollywood films and reality TV.

Low key lighting

Low key lighting has dark shadows in stark contrast to the lighter parts of the frame. This creates a serious and dramatic atmosphere commonly used in thriller, horror and crime drama.

The stark low key lighting in this shot helps to create an eerie atmosphere. Along with the use of a long shot, the overall mise-en-scène suggests isolation of the character.

Intensity and levels

Light intensity and **levels** help to create mood. High intensity lighting creates a light bright scene with soft shadows and may be used in many different scenes. Low light levels will help to build curiosity or suspense.

Audio

Audio is a very important component of media products, be they radio broadcasts, television programmes, computer games or film.

Soundtrack

Soundtracks are used to add emotional depth to TV programmes and films.

For instance, low strings may suggest suspense and tension, whilst loud brass instruments, and percussion will add excitement and power to an action scene.

2. Two photographs, **A** and **B**, have been created to use in an advert in a magazine. Compare and contrast how lighting has been used to contribute to the mise-en-scène in the photographs. [4]

3. Explain **one** way that audio could enhance walking through a peaceful forest in a computer game. [2]

2. *Photo A makes use of warm lighting[1] which evokes feelings of drama and power.[1] The black background suggests the perfume is for evening use/leads to romance.[1] Lighting has also been put behind the bottle[1] to highlight the warmth of the bottle colour.[1] By contrast, photo B uses high key lighting[1] implying it is light and fresh.[1] The simplicity of the photo and background suggests an elegant and fashionable style.[1]*

3. *Sound effects[1] could be used for the footsteps / birds / wind in the trees.[1] A sound track using woodwind / flutes / panpipes[1] would help to create a relaxed emotion in the player of the game.[1]*

Sound effects

Many sounds such as a creaking door, walking on snow or a dog barking won't be recorded on a set. Instead, these sounds will be recorded separately by a **Foley artist** and mixed by the sound editor. Sound effects help to bring props and movement to life.

Sometimes **silence** will be used to add tension to a scene.

Sound effects are particularly important in computer games as they react to the movements of a player and help to create an immersive experience.

Music genre

The **genre** of music used will make a big difference to the mood of a media product. For instance, a dramatic film score may be used to create suspense in a war film.

Dialogue

An audio technician will need to make sure that what actors say is clearly recorded. **Dialogue** is usually recorded using audio recording equipment and microphones separate from any film or video cameras.

Vocal intonation

In radio broadcasts and podcasts, people will make use of **vocal intonation** to make the recording sound interesting. This is especially true of voice over artists which may be used in products including advertising and documentaries.

INTERACTIVITY AND ANIMATION

Interactivity

Interactivity is a two-way interaction between the users and the media product. Interactivity can be found in a wide range of digital products including computer games, apps, websites, and social media platforms.

If the end user is actively involved in the product, it will be more engaging and is likely to be used for a longer period of time.

Websites

Websites are all interactive products. They contain features such as buttons, hotspots, rollovers and hyperlinks. They can also include audio and video content that a user can stream via an embedded media player.

Apps

Apps have a huge range of interactive features. For example, an app could include augmented reality so you can 'try before you buy' for products such as furniture.

A navigation app makes use of a user's location to indicate their position on a map.

Animation

Animation is the combination of a series of still images to create a moving image. Computer animation is used in a variety of media products including advertising, websites, apps, gaming, education, television, and film.

Animation makes a product more engaging for the audience and also entertains. The design of the animation will differ depending on the target audience and purpose of the product.

For younger children, animations are simple in their design and may use predominantly primary colours. Older audiences might expect animations to be more realistic, especially within gaming.

1. A website makes use of interactive rollover buttons for users to choose products.
   Identify **two** other interactive features that may be used in a website. [2]

2. Explain how the use of interactive buttons could increase user engagement. [2]

   1. *Hyperlink,[1] forms / text boxes,[1] hotspots,[1] video player controls.[1]*

   2. *The rollover button's graphic will change as the user hovers over it.[1] This may make use of shadows and lighting effects[1] so that it feels more like a real button.[1] A click / sound effect could be added to the button[1] that makes it 'feel' more authentic to the user.[1] Animation could be used on the button[1] to help draw the user's eye towards it.[1]*

EXAMINATION PRACTICE

You are working as a graphic designer. You have been asked to design the cover of a fiction book aimed at 11–15-year-olds called The Secret Island. The story is about three 15-year-old friends who discover a secret island and encounter scary bears, dogs and a hermit whilst searching for treasure.

(a) Explain **one** purpose of a book cover.   [2]

(b) Other than age, identify **two** other ways the target audience for this book can be segmented. [2]

(c) Describe how the graphics used on the cover may reflect the age group of the audience.   [2]

Before finalising the design, a market research company has been asked to carry out some research with the target audience about book covers they like from the same genre.

(d) Identify **one** method of primary research that could be used.   [1]

(e) Describe how the method you chose in part (d) would be used to carry out the research.   [3]

(f) Outline **one** benefit for the graphic designer in making use of the market research when designing the cover.   [2]

You have been asked to create a short promotional video to be shared via social media. The video needs to impart the child's excitement at reading the book.

(g) Explain **one** camera shot that could be used to give the feeling of excitement in the promotional video.   [2]

The video will also be added to a website that promotes the book. The publisher of the book is keen that the website is interactive.

(h) Identify **two** interactive features of a website.   [2]

Below is the final book cover.

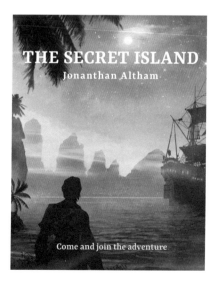

(i) Describe how the colour and positioning of elements in the layout have been used to help promote the book.   [4]

WORK PLANS

Components

Work plans are used to plan out the different elements that need to be completed within a project. In a media product there are three **phases** that would need to be covered in the work plan:

- **pre-production** (planning)
- **production** (creating)
- **post-production** (editing and reviewing)

Work plans list all the tasks that need to be done to complete a project. They also show the project start and end dates, as well as when the different components should be completed so that the project finishes on time.

Resources

Resources include the hardware, software and people required to complete the project.

Timescales

The time given to each activity and task in the project.

Milestones

Milestones are the dates when key parts of the project are complete.

Tasks

Tasks are the main phases of the project such as pre-production, production, and post-production in a film. In other media projects they may include planning, creation and review phases.

Workflow

This is the order in which activities are completed. Activities may have **dependencies**. This means that other activities need to be completed first.

Activities

Tasks are broken down into **activities**. These are the smaller components that need to be carried out to complete the task. They are also known as **sub-tasks**.

Contingencies

Contingencies are a back up plan for when problems occur. This is spare time allocated in the plan to allow for the unexpected.

Workplans may be represented differently.
For instance:

- Milestones may be shown as a symbol such as a diamond.
- Contingency time may be shaded like activities, but use a different colour.

Uses and benefits of a work plan

A work plan helps manage tasks, activities, time and resources in any type of media product. The benefits of a work plan include:

- Ensuring that timescales and deadlines are clear so that the project can be completed on time.

- Assisting with the allocation of resources, so you know what equipment and people are needed and when.

- Planning what to do if there are issues to make sure the project can still be finished on time and in budget.

A workplan has been created for the production of an advertising poster.

Task	Activities	Mar				Apr			
		Wk 1	Wk 2	Wk 3	Wk 4	Wk 5	Wk 6	Wk 7	Wk 8
Plan campaign	Identify client requirements								
Milestone – Planning complete									
Poster design and creation	Create visualisation diagram								
	Identify resources / assets								
	Check for any permissions								
	Review draft poster								
	Create / prepare assets								
	Create poster layout								
Milestone – Poster design complete									
Review	Sent poster to client								
	Make amendments								
	Client approval								
	Prepare files for printer								
Review complete – Poster ready for print									

(a) Weeks 4 and 6 are blank. Identify what this represents. [1]

(b) Explain **two** ways in which workflow is shown in the workplan. [4]

(c) Explain **two** advantages of creating the work plan for the design team. [4]

(a) *Contingency time.[1]*

(b) *Tasks/activities are listed in the order that they will be carried out[1] so that the phases of the project can clearly be seen.[1] Activities that can be carried out at the same time / concurrently[1] are indicated as being highlighted in the same week.[1] By running tasks concurrently, the project can be completed sooner.[1]*
Task/activity dependencies are indicated by black arrows.[1] These allow people working on the project to understand which tasks/activities need to be completed[1] before a particular task/activity can be started.[1]
Accept other appropriate answers.

(c) *Work plans help manage time[1] because they give clear timescales for when things need to be completed by.[1] Work plans help manage resources[1] because they help to identify the hardware, software and people needed.[1]*

MIND MAPS

A **mind map**, or spider diagram, is a way to plan out thoughts and ideas in an organised way. A mind map can be **created digitally** or be **hand drawn**.

Purpose of a mind map

- The purpose of a mind map is to outline ideas quickly.
- A mind map also shows the connections between different ideas.

Use of a mind map

A mind map will normally be used at the beginning of a project, for example, to analyse a client brief. At this stage it allows an overview of all the components of the project to be considered. Mind maps may also be a useful way to generate ideas on one task required in the project.

Mind maps may have many users in the team. For example, a campaign manager could create a set of ideas for a promotional campaign. They would then share these with the wider team to generate discussion. Once all the ideas are complete, team members could carry out further planning. For instance, a designer may make a visualisation diagram of a poster that will be created for the campaign.

See **page 86** & **87** for examples of mind maps.

Content of a mind map

- A mind map consists of the **main** or **central idea** in the middle.
- **Nodes** are connected to the main idea by lines called **branches**. These show how the ideas are related to each other.
- **Sub-nodes** are connected to the nodes to help organise the ideas more clearly.
- Each **node** or **sub-node** includes text and/ or images.

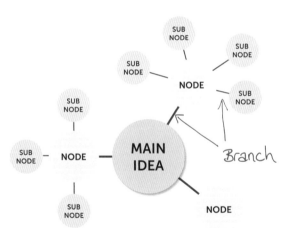

1. (a) A digital mind map is being created for the production of a leaflet.
   Identify **two** items of hardware that will be required to produce it. [2]
   (b) Describe how a hand drawn mind map could be digitised. [2]

1. (a) *Computer system / PC / desktop / laptop / tablet,[1] mouse,[1] keyboard,[1] display/monitor.[1]*
   (b) *A photo could be taken with a digital camera/phone camera[1] and transferred to a computer via SD card / email attachment / Bluetooth transfer.[1]*
   The paper copy could be scanned[1] using a scanner.[1]

MOOD BOARDS

A mood board is a planning document that assembles a range of materials in order to reflect the potential style of a media product.

Examples of colour, graphics, typography and texture may all be included. These may be **physical**, (such as photos, pages cut out from a magazine and texture samples), or created digitally. Remember, that even a **digital** mood board could contain photos of textures and physical objects.

Purpose of a mood board

The purpose of a mood board is to develop the feeling and style of the product. It assists in giving ideas for the later planning stages, such as the creation of a visualisation diagram or storyboard. It may also be referred to when producing the final media product. Mood boards can also be used to get feedback from a client or the rest of the design team on a particular style.

Skate Park Promotion Campaign   Board 1

2. (a) Simon is a web developer who has been asked to create a website for a client. Simon has decided to include a colour scheme on a digital mood board.

   Name **two** other types of media that Simon could include on his mood board.   [2]

   (b) Other than Simon, explain **two** other people who may make use of the mood board.   [2]

3. Identify **two** features that could be on a digital mood board but not a physical one.   [2]

   2. (a) Two from: Photographs,[1] examples of typography/text style,[1] graphics,[1] illustrations,[1] photos of textures.[1]

   (b) Two from: A photographer,[1] a graphic designer,[1] an illustrator,[1] the client.[1]

   3. Two from: Videos,[1] audio,[1] animation.[1]

Content of a mood board

The content of a mood board will differ depending on whether it is physical or digital.

Physical mood board

A **physical** mood board will be produced on a large piece of paper or card and contain materials such as photographs, pages cut out from a magazine, fabrics, examples of text showing typography, and colour swatches.

Digital mood board

A **digital** mood board may include digital images, graphics, text, videos and audio files.

Digital mood boards are made in a wide range of software. They are typically exported as PDFs or JPG images for easy access and distribution.

SCRIPTS

Purpose of a script

A **script** is a written document used for media products such as a TV drama, documentaries, television or radio advertising, news, or film.

Content and conventions of a script

Scripts typically contain the following information:

Scene information

Technical information such as transitions, shot, and camera movement are often included

Sound effects

Dialogue (what is being said)

Location description

Character names

Scripts have a number of conventions that make them easier to read and understand for the variety of people that will need to use them.

Dialogue is indented under the character's name.

Scripts usually use **Courier** font – this is a monospace font meaning each letter has the same width.

Capitals are used for character names and scene headings.

Bold is used for, actions, emotion or emphasis.

Scene headings use abbreviations such as EXT (exterior) or INT (interior). The location and time may be used in a scene heading. V.O. is used for voice overs.

Speech direction may be given in brackets.

Use of a script

The script is a crucial document to the production team.

A director will use the script to develop their overall vision for the production. It is their job to interpret the script and bring it to life on the screen.

An actor or presenter will use a script so that they know what to say, when to say it and how to say it. They will also know how to move or behave whilst on the set or location. These are known as stage directions or blocking.

The script contains the outline of the shot types and camera movement. This will be used to plan the required shots and equipment needed for each scene.

The production designer will use the script to plan the set and props required for the production.

The costume designer will use the script to dress the cast in suitable clothing.

Look at the script below.

1. Label A in the script shows a transition. Identify the features of a script labelled B–E. [4]
2. Identify the meaning of the abbreviations INT and EXT. [2]
3. Later in the script, the abbreviation V.O. is used. Explain why a sound engineer would be interested in this part of the script. [1]

1. *B: Location;[1] C: Character name;[1] D: Shot type;[1] E: Dialogue.[1]*
2. *INT means interior (inside).[1] EXT means exterior (outside).[1]*
3. *V.O. means voice over[1]. The sound engineer would need to record this part separately to the other parts of the script that would be filmed.[1]*

STORYBOARDS

Purpose of a storyboard

A **storyboard** is a series of drawings, usually with brief directions, showing the sequence of shots needed in a film or television program. Some computer games may also make use of storyboards.

Use of a storyboard

A storyboard will be used by the production team to see what is happening scene by scene in a visual way. Technical details such as camerawork, sounds and lighting will be considered based on the instructions and feeling given by the script and storyboard.

They are a vital document for different people in the production team.

The **director** uses the storyboard as a visual blueprint for the whole film or video in sequence.	The **director of photography** and **camera operators** use the storyboard to understand the required camera angles and movement.	Members of the production team and actors may see the parts of the storyboard that are related to their role.

Content and conventions of a storyboard

A storyboard will contain a sketch for each shot or scene as well as technical details such as:

Timings and number of scenes

Scenes are rarely shot in order as each scene might have different locations and camera setup required. Scenes may be made up of more than one shot. Timings may be given for each scene.

Camera shots and movement

Details about camera angles and movement help the camera crew plan the equipment that is needed including whether a dolly and track or tripod are required to capture the shot.

Location

The storyboard provides information on where filming will take place, either in a studio or on location. The location department will use this to scout out appropriate places that may be used for filming, carry out a location recce and conduct risk assessments to check whether they are suitable.

Sound

The sound crew will use the storyboard to plan any dialogue that needs to be recorded during the production phase, as well as sound effects and background music that need to be added in during post-production.

The Race

Scene 1 – Shot 1

Establishing shot, title wipes in
Runners poised to start race
(not a sprint race)

Scene 2 – Shot 1

Runner X looking focused

Scene 2 – Shot 2

Three second pause on starting
pistol.
Pistol fired – Cut to

Scene 2 – Shot 3

Race starts – Runners jostling
to inside lane – Cut to

Scene 2 – Shot 4

Runner falls – Dissolve to

Scene 2 – Shot 5

Race continues in background,
stricken runner is helped by
track officials – Cut to

1. The above storyboard is for a film called 'The Race'. It is about a runner that overcomes adversity before winning the final race.

   Identify **two** members of the production crew who are likely to be interested in seeing the storyboard before filming scene 2, shot 4 in the above storyboard. [2]

2. (a) Explain why scene numbers are included on a storyboard. [2]

   (b) Other than scene numbers and a sketch, identify **three** items of information that might be included in a storyboard. [3]

   1. *The director,[1] the director of photography,[1] the camera operator,[1] the stunt man falling.[1]*

   2. (a) *Scene numbers are used because scenes are not always filmed in order[1] so it makes it easier to put the scenes in the correct order[1] during the post-production (editing) phase.[1]*

      (b) *Camera angles,[1] camera shot types,[1] camera movements,[1] transitions,[1] duration/timing,[1] sound effects,[1] location,[1] voice over.[1]*

VISUALISATION DIAGRAMS

Purpose of a visualisation diagram

A **visualisation diagram** is a rough sketch of a media product. The purpose of a visualisation diagram is to indicate or give a representation of how the final product will look including the content, layout, font and colour.

Use of a visualisation diagram

A visualisation diagram is often used to show the design team what the product might look like. It could be discussed and changed if needed. It is also a useful method of sharing design ideas with the client. The client can then propose changes to the design if they are not happy with it.

It is best used for products that are static (non-moving) such as magazines, posters, DVD and Blu-ray covers, book covers, leaflets and brochures. They can also be used for a single screen in a computer game, such as a menu screen, and a web page design.

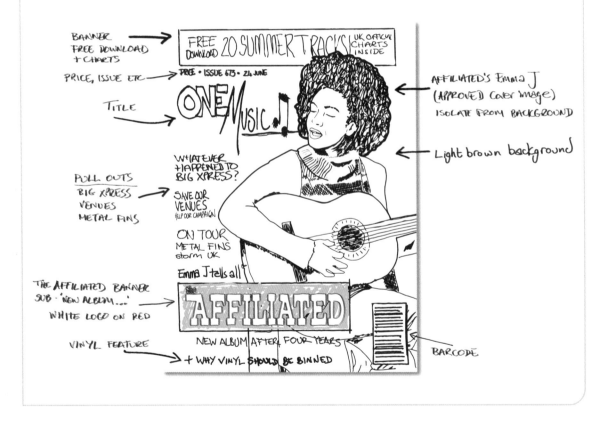

Content of a visualisation diagram

A good visualisation diagram should contain enough detail that a graphic designer could create the product using it. They can be digital, or hand drawn but should include the following features:

Sketches of the content

Key photos and graphics should have a detailed sketch rather than a labelled box.

! Note

A quick sketch of the photo, graphic or logo gives the designer lots more information to work from than a labelled box.

Layout and positioning

The diagram should clearly show how photos, graphics and text are positioned. This includes areas that are intentionally left blank.

Annotation

These are labels around the visualisation diagram that provide further information about the design. These should include detail of the planned colours, typography and justifications for any design elements

Specific features for the media product

A visualisation diagram should reflect what would be seen on the final product so will need to include typical features of that type of product. For example, a magazine front cover would contain a barcode and issue number whilst a computer game cover would contain a PEGI rating.

1. Explain the purpose of a visualisation diagram. [2]

2. A local café is opening in a month's time and is going to be running a marketing campaign for its launch. You have been asked to create the pre-production documents for the launch poster.
   Identify **three** items you would find on the visualisation diagram for the launch poster. [3]

   1. *The purpose of a visualisation diagram is to show the intended layout[1] of the final product.[1]*

   2. *Images / graphics / photos,[1] text,[1] annotations,[1] title,[1] layout / positioning,[1] colour scheme.[1]*

WIREFRAMES

Purpose of wireframes

A **wireframe** is a planning document that shows the layout and functionality of interactive products such as apps or websites. It also shows how different webpages or screens link to one another.

Use of wireframes

Web developers and web designers will make use of a wireframe to help program and design a website.

Content and conventions of a wireframe

Wireframes show the design of each screen or web page including images and videos, text and navigational features. They may also include annotation to explain the user's journey between the different elements and justify design choices.

Unlike a visualisation diagram, they do not include sketches to show what the images would look like. Instead, a box with a cross in it represents and image, whilst straight lines represent text.

Wireframes may be created by hand on paper. Specialist software allows the easy creation of digital wireframes. Some basic interactivities may also be possible in digital wireframes. This may allow ideas to be considered with other team members of test users.

1. (a) Identify **two** media products that might use a wireframe in the pre-production stage. [2]
   (b) Describe how a wireframe can be used to plan an app. [3]

   (a) Website,[1] app,[1] multimedia / information kiosk,[1] computer or digital game.[1]

   (b) A wireframe clearly shows the layout of the different screens of the app[1] so it is easy to see where content is positioned[1] in relation to the page.[1] A wireframe can be used to show the functionality of the app[1] by showing navigational features,[1] and the path they take the user on.[1] Images can be represented by a square containing a cross[1] and text can be represented by straight lines.[1]

ASSET LOGS

Purpose of asset logs

When making media products, you must have permission to use media assets such as images or video clips. An **asset log** is a list of all of the assets used in a media product.

An asset log will include details of the file, such as the filename, where it will be used and the source such as the website or image library where it was found. It also includes information about whether permission is required from the copyright holder and whether it has been given.

A simple table may be used to make an assets log. Large media companies are likely to have specialist software to record assets that have been used along with the asset licence.

	A	B	C	D	E	F	G
1	Asset ID	Filename	Description	Properties	Source	Legal issues	Use
2	1	lion.jpg	Lion in black and white with yellow eyes	640 × 448px	www.shutterstock.com Image ref: 1934666582	Image library – need to agree type of use and pay fee. Once permission is given, the image is released without a watermark	DVD front cover (main image)
3	2	lion cub.jpg	Lion cub isolated	6720 × 4480px	www.alamy.com Image ref: 151048639	Image library – need to agree the type of use and pay fee	DVD back cover
4	3	fur texture.jpg	My own photo of fur texture of black rug	1920 × 1080px	Original photo taken by myself	I own the copyright	DVD back cover
5	4	zoo lions.jpg	Photo of lions in zoo	1024 × 768px	Original photo taken by friend	Permission granted (signed release). No Zoo branding visible.	DVD back cover image in box

2. (a) A designer downloads a photograph from a website which they plan to use on a poster. One item of information they will record about the photograph is the permitted use. Give **two** other items of information that may be recorded. [2]

(b) Describe how an image downloaded from a website may be used legally. [2]

(a) The filename/asset ID,[1] a description of the image,[1] properties of the image / resolution / dimensions / filetype,[1] the source of the image / hyperlink to the image,[1] where the image is used / what project the image is used in.[1]

(b) A licence to use the image[1] may be purchased.[1]

The image may have a free use licence / Creative Commons licence[1] in which case the conditions of the licence should be checked and recorded.[1]

A request for permission may be made to the website owner,[1] once they have given permission, this will be recorded and the image may be used.[1]

It is crucial for media companies to record the details of any media assets such as images or video used. They also need to record any licences and what permissions have been given.

Failure to use assets legally could result in a breach of copyright legislation.

FLOW CHARTS

Purpose of flow charts

A **flow chart** is a diagram that represents a workflow or series of processes. It offers a clear step-by-step approach including decisions that may be made along the way and their outcomes.

Use of flow charts

A flow chart might be used to map out how an end user might move through a website or show what happens when choices are made within a computer game.

Flow charts are technical documents that may be used by web developers, web designers, games programmers and games developers.

Content and conventions used in flow charts

Flow charts use a standard set of symbols to represent different stages within a system. Each box is connected by an arrow to show the direction of flow.

The most commonly used features are shown here:

Decision   No →

↓ Yes

A **decision** symbol poses a question with a Yes or No answer. The response determines which arrow will be followed. It is important that arrows coming out of decision symbols are labelled.

Start / End

The **terminator** symbol is used at the beginning and end of a flow chart to show where it starts and finishes.

Input / Output

Input and **output** symbols show what will be entered by the user or what will be output to the screen.

Process

The **process** box shows a step in the process. Details of the steps are included inside the box.

Arrows are used to connect the symbols and show the direction of flow through the flow chart.

A fashion shop has decided that it wants to expand by selling clothes online.

A flow diagram has been created to show the process of logging in to the website.

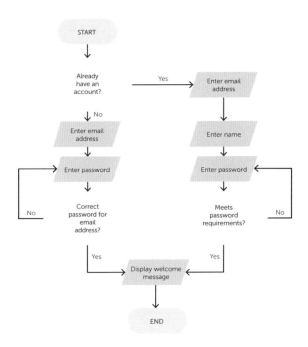

1. Identify a job role that may make use of the flow chart. [1]
2. The flowchart shows how a user may register a new account or log in to an existing account. Give **one** difference between these two processes. [1]
3. Explain **one** benefit of using flow charts to plan the functionality of a website. [2]

1. *Web designer,[1] web developer.[1]*

2. *To register an account, the user also needs to 'Enter name'.[1]*

   When registering an account, the password is checked against password requirements. When logging in, the password is checked to see if it matched the one stored for the email address.[1]

3. *It will be easier/faster to make changes to a flow chart than a final website.[1] This will save time later, as the web developer/web designer is likely to get the processes correct first time.[1]*

   The flow chart will give an exact plan of the processes required[1] meaning that all people working on the project will understand how it works[1] leading to fewer mistakes / less need to alter work at a later date.[1]

LEGAL ISSUES PROTECTING INDIVIDUALS

Privacy and permissions

In the UK, there is no law preventing people from taking photographs or recording video in public places. However, for **commercial** purposes, you may need to get **permission** and pay a fee.

If you are using **private property** as a location, you will always need to obtain the correct permission. Private property is not just houses and stately homes, but also includes shopping centres, railway stations, offices and many more.

Photographers may be hired to shoot specific photographs or may upload their work to image libraries for purchase. As they have the rights to the photos, they will allow certain permissions.

The following are some possible examples of permissions given in different situations:

Situation: A wedding and family portrait photographer.

Permissions: Some will not give permission to copy the photographs and may charge for each copy. Other photographers may charge a fee for each photo and give the original digital photo with permission to create as many copies or prints as wanted.

Situation: A photographer takes photos as a hobby. They have shared their photos with a Creative Commons licence.

Permissions: The Creative Commons licence will need to be checked. Some images will only allow personal use, whilst others will allow commercial use. Usually no fee will be charged for using the image, but it's important to check that the person sharing the photo has the right to share it and model release forms if necessary.

Situation: A photograph has been taken of a model for use in advertising on a billboard.

Permissions: The model will need to give their permission to use the photographs by signing a **model release form**.

Situation: A photograph of people on a busy street is available on a photographic library that states 'for editorial use only'.

Permissions: The photograph may not be used for commercial purposes such as advertising. This is because the people walking on the street won't have given their permission to be photographed. However, the photograph may be used for news and education, such as in a newspaper but cannot be edited or manipulated. To do this, a **fee** is paid to purchase a **license** to use the image.

Invasion of privacy and harassment

Photographers need to make sure that they are respectful and don't **invade people's privacy**. They also need to be careful that they don't pressure or intimidate people they are taking photographs of. This is known as **harassment**.

For the exam you do not need to know the specific laws (Acts or legislation) that apply to privacy, defamation and data protection.

Defamation

Defamation is when damage is caused to the character and reputation of an individual or a company by a statement or action that is untrue. **Libel** and **slander** are two forms of defamation.

Libel

Libel is when a false statement is published. This could be an article or photograph in a newspaper, magazine, television program or even a social media post. In libel, the defamation is permanent - for instance, a newspaper article will still be available to read next year.

Slander

Slander uses a temporary form of defamation. This typically happens with speech.

Data protection

Data protection aims to protect a person's personal data. The rights of the person, known as a data subject, are that the data is:

- Used for a specific purpose
- Relevant and not more than needed
- Accurate and kept up to date
- Not kept longer than necessary
- Stored securely

For instance, a media company may need to store the personal information of a model they use in an advertisement. They would only be able to ask for the information they need, such as their name, contact details and the permissions that were agreed. This would need to be stored securely.

Intellectual property rights

Photographs, graphics, video, logos, **ideas** and **patents** are all forms of **intellectual property**. They are protected from being copied without permission using **copyright**. There are some permitted uses when you may still copy materials, such as for private study. This is known as **fair use**.

Photographs, graphics, video, music and text are all protected by copyright.

This prevents others from using the media without permission. It allows media producers to charge to view or re-use media products.

Copyright uses the © symbol, whilst **Creative Commons** licenses use the symbol on the right.

Patents may be registered for inventions. These will have a clever or unique idea to solve a problem.

Logos and product names are examples of trademarks. Companies will be very careful about how their trademarks are used.

A **trademark** is instead indicated by using the trademark symbol ™. The trademark may be registered, in which case the registered trademark symbol ® is used.

You are a graphic designer working on a new leaflet to promote the opening of a new nightclub. You have found an image on a stock image library of a crowd dancing to music.

(a) The image has a watermark. Describe the use of watermarks on stock images.   [3]

(b) Identify **one** type of permission that the licence for the image will need to include.   [1]

(a) The image has text or a logo placed over it [1] which makes the image unusable in the leaflet. [1] When a fee is paid for a licence, [1] a high resolution image without the watermark is made available for the user to download. [1]

(b) The right to use the image commercially / in advertising, [1] a model release form, [1] the right to use the photo on a printed leaflet. [1]

REGULATION AND CERTIFICATION

The media industry is regulated by several different bodies. It is their job to make sure that media products that are published, broadcast and distributed follow certain rules and regulations.

Regulatory organisations

ASA (Advertising Standards Authority)

- The **ASA** is the regulator for advertising in all forms of media, from TV and radio to billboards, magazines and adverts on the Internet, smartphones, and tablets.
- They make sure that adverts conform to the Advertising Codes.
- They regulate and act on complaints and make sure that adverts are not misleading, harmful or offensive.

Ofcom (The Office of Communications)

- **Ofcom** is the regulator for communication services including television, radio, broadband, telephone and mobile services.
- Their role includes looking at complaints from viewers or listeners and checking if the broadcaster has broken any rules within the Broadcasting Code.
- They also make sure that programmes broadcast are not harmful or offensive.

Classification systems and certifications

BBFC certifications

- The **BBFC** (British Board of Film Classification) is responsible for classifying films and trailers that are screened in the cinema or sold on DVD/Blu-Ray.
- Special symbols are used on posters, DVD/Blu-Ray covers which help show which age group a film is suitable for.

PEGI certifications

- **PEGI** (Pan European Game Information) is a game content rating system that uses age recommendations and content descriptors so that people can make informed choices when buying games. PEGI ratings are for both the UK and Europe.
- Age labels are used to show the minimum age that each game is suitable for.

BBFC classifications

U – Universal; suitable for all.

PG – Parental guidance – Parents should consider whether the content is suitable for younger children.

12A – Suitable for 12+. May be seen by younger children if accompanied by an adult.

12, 15, 18 – Suitable for 12+, 15+ and 18+ respectively.

A film production is complete and ready to be shown to audiences in cinemas and on television.

(a) Describe the role of the BBFC in the film release. [2]

(b) The film will be shown on television with advertisement breaks. Complete the sentence.

The A_____ S_____ A_____ will be responsible for regulating the advertisements. [1]

(a) *The BBFC will watch the film[1] and give it a classification.[1] A BBFC age-rating symbol will be put on posters/marketing materials.[1] Cinemas should restrict the customers that can see the film (if it's a 12A, 12, 15 or 18 certificate).[1]*

(b) *Advertising Standards Authority.[1]*

HEALTH AND SAFETY

During all phases of a media production, any **health and safety risks** and **hazards** must be considered. Workers need to be mindful of hazards whether they are working at a computer, using photographic equipment or working on a film or television production.

Examples of risks in television or film production

Moving objects

There are many ways that objects move to create hazards, for example, a camera may move through the air on a crane or a car chase scene may need to be filmed.

Reducing the risk of harm

- Get permission to close roads or walkways as appropriate.
- Make sure operators of cranes are trained and certified.

Carrying heavy equipment

Care needs to be taken when transporting heavy equipment such as lighting or cameras.

Reducing the risk of harm

- Equipment is transported in flight cases that may have wheels.
- Staff are trained in how to safely move equipment.

Trip hazards

Equipment, such as lighting, will have many electric cables. A track for a dolly camera will also cause a tripping hazard.

Reducing the risk of harm

- Cable protectors, mats and ramps cover cables so that people can safely walk over the cables.
- Cables will be taped down with gaffer tape (thick and strong tape).

Electrocution

If devices fail or are incorrectly wired, they may create a risk of electrocution.

Reducing the risk of harm

- Maintain equipment.
- Only use qualified and trained crew.
- Protect cables from being cut or damaged.

Examples of risks when using computers

Neck/back problems

Having displays at incorrect heights or sitting with bad posture may lead to serious back or neck problems.

Reducing the risk of harm

- Have the display directly in front of the chair to prevent twisting.
- Use a fully adjustable chair.
- Have the display at eye level.

Eye strain

Looking at a display for a long time may result in headaches and aching eyes.

Reducing the risk of harm

- Look away every 20 mins.
- Take longer breaks every 2 hours.
- Use the computer in a well lit room.

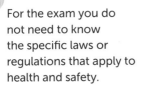

For the exam you do not need to know the specific laws or regulations that apply to health and safety.

RECCES AND RISK ASSESSMENTS

Location recce

A **recce** is a visit to a location that might be used for photography, filming or recording. The purpose of the visit is:

- To check the safety of the site, that the site is accessible and that permission to use the site can be obtained.
- Check sound issues – for example, is there any background noise such as heavy traffic.
- Check lighting issues – for example, a large building may block the sun from reaching the location, additional lighting will be required.
- Check facilities, such as toilets and parking areas.
- Decide which shots and camera movement will work with the location.

Detailed notes will be made and a series of photographs will be taken to show the potential location from all angles and times of day for reference. This provides information on the suitability of the location and helps to establish if there are any issues with safety and access that need to be incorporated into a risk assessment.

A scene for a television comedy is going to be filmed on location at the front of a house.

(a) Explain how a recce may be used in planning the lighting of the location. [2]

(b) Explain the purpose of a risk assessment before filming takes place. [2]

(a) It will be possible to see the direction of the sun / where shadows are cast / obstructions such as trees[1] so that the crew know what additional lighting will be required.[1]

(b) A risk assessment identifies potential risks and harm[1] and suggests steps to reduce them.[1]

Risk assessment

Anywhere where media people work, including where crew, actors or the public will be affected, must have a **risk assessment**. This is a document that identifies potential risks, their likelihood, the harm associated with the risk and how each risk will be reduced.

Example Risk Assessment form

Activity *What are you doing?*	Hazard *What might cause danger or injury?*	Risk *What risks are there from the hazard? Who is at risk?*	Controls *What measures will be in place to reduce the risk?*	Probability (P) 1–5	Severity (S) 1–5	Risk rating (P × S)
Transporting equipment to a park.	Equipment could be dropped, create a trip hazard or physical injury.	Broken bones, bruises, concussion, fatality if equipment falls from a height.	Use flight cases and trolleys. Multiple people used to lift heavy items.	2	3	6

EXAMINATION PRACTICE

A new magazine is being launched called 'Mountain Biking'. The magazine will be aimed at an adventurous and active audience of teenagers and young adults that enjoy cycling off-road and don't have a problem getting muddy.

(a) A workplan has been created for the creation of the front cover of the magazine. Using the work plan below, identify the parts of a work plan that are represented by labels A, B and C. [3]

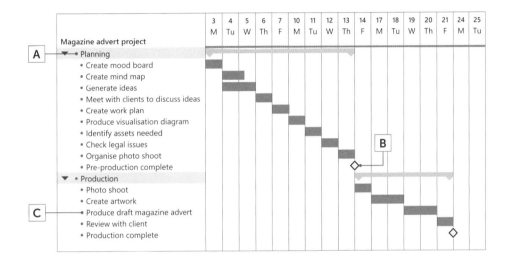

(b) Outline how a graphic designer could use a work plan to help manage a project. [3]

(c) One activity that needs to be carried out is checking any legal issues with the assets that are needed for the cover.

Explain **two** legal issues that may need to be considered. [4]

(d) When sourcing images for the final magazine advert, four different symbols were given next to various image. Identify the meaning of each symbol by completing the table. The first symbol has been identified for you. [3]

Symbol found	Meaning
©	Copyright
TM	
®	
CC	

This mind map has been created to help develop ideas for the design of the magazine.

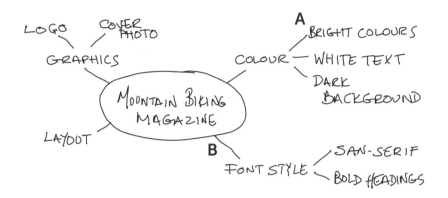

(e) Identify the **two** parts of the mind map, labelled **A** and **B**. [2]

(f) Describe the purpose of a mind map. [2]

You have been asked to create a mood board for the magazine.

(g) Identify **four** items that could be included on a digital mood board. [4]

(h) Identify **one** potential user for the mood board. [1]

Parts of the magazine are regulated by the ASA.

(i) State which part of the magazine the ASA is responsible for. [1]

The magazine has a website that allows people to sign up to receive email updates about the launch.

(j) Explain **one** action that the magazine publishers will need to take to be compliant with data protection legislation. [2]

(k) The magazine publisher's website will automatically send emails to users who register. Appropriate emails are sent in response to the links that have been clicked on by the subscriber.

Identify a suitable document that could be given to the web developer to help them program the email marketing system. [1]

Fig.1 is a draft of a **visualisation** diagram for the magazine front cover.

Fig. 1

(l) Create an improved version of the draft visualisation diagram in **Fig.1**.   [9]

Marks will be awarded for:
- Relevant components and conventions used
- Layout
- Annotations that explain how the improvements better meet the client's requirements.

The magazine publisher will also be creating a short video which will play on their website. This will help to entice the users into signing up to their mailing list.

Fig. 2 shows a draft of the storyboard that the video editor will use to create the website video.

Fig. 2

| Mountain Biker flies off jump | Biker shown from front as they fly through the air and land | Wheel slides in muddy puddle | Logo and call to action appear |

(m) Discuss the suitability of the storyboard (**Fig. 2**) for use by the video editor.   [9]

Marks will be awarded for:
- Suggesting changes that improve the storyboard.
- Explaining how the changes you suggest will make the storyboard more effective for the video editor.

DISTRIBUTING MEDIA PRODUCTS

Media products need to be **distributed** to customers. This may take place through an online platform, such as a television streaming service, or through physical media, such as a DVD.

Physical platforms

Physical platforms are the specific devices that are used to play or show media products. They include **computers**, **interactive TV**, information **kiosks** and **mobile devices**.

Physical media

Certain media products might be distributed via physical media such as **compact discs (CD)**, **Digital Versatile Discs (DVD)** and **Blu-ray**. Removable media such as **memory sticks** may be used to share large files within a media organisation without the need to upload and download.

Paper-based methods are most useful for distributing physical magazines, newspapers, brochures, and leaflets. Increasingly however, there are digital versions available of these.

Online

Media products such as games are downloaded as **apps** from an app store or marketplace. They are then installed onto devices such as tablets or smartphones. Some apps will stop working if the Internet connection to a device is lost.

Multimedia content is distributed through several methods. For instance, music may be purchased to download or stream through services such as iTunes®, Amazon Music® and Spotify®. Video and film are distributed via apps such as such as BBC iPlayer® or NetFlix®.

Websites are also used to distribute media products. For example, a car manufacturer may offer a brochure to be downloaded from their website. Music, video and multimedia may all be distributed via websites. One advantage of companies using their own websites is that they will be in complete control of the media product and how it is presented. However, they will usually have a much smaller audience.

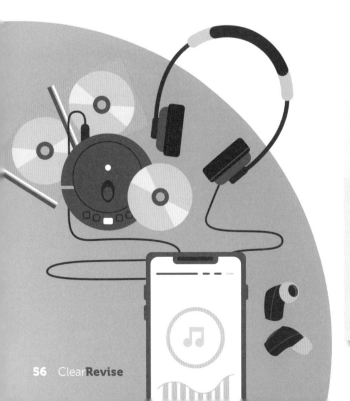

1. Explain **one** potential issue of using physical media to distribute a product.   [2]
2. Give **one** advantage for a band in choosing to release their new album on a streaming music service rather than a CD.   [1]

1. *Physical media could easily get lost / damaged[1] so you would no longer have access to that media product.[1]*

2. *More customers will be able to listen to the album on devices such as smartphones / tablets.[1]*

   The cost of distribution will probably be lower[1] (as there is no need to make the CD and no postage costs).

FILE COMPRESSION

Some files, such as video, music or images are very large. This requires lots of storage space to save. Compression is used to reduce the size of a file. There are two types of compression: **lossy** and **lossless**.

Types of compression

Original
uncompressed image

File size 739 kB

Lossy compression
(JPG)

File size 4 kB

Lossless compression
(PNG)

File size 72 kB

Lossy compression

Lossy compression can be applied to graphics, photos, videos and music. It can result in a significant reduction in the file size, but it will lose some of the original information. If an image is over compressed, too much information is lost and errors will be noticeable. The lossy compression above has resulted in **digital artefacts** such as **pixelation** and incorrect colours.

- Image file formats include JPG

- Audio file formats include MP3, and AAC

- Video file formats include MPEG 2, MPEG 4 / MP4 and H.264

Lossless compression

Lossless compression can be used on text files, zip files, photos, music and video. No information is lost when the file is compressed. This is the only way to compress files such as text documents or computer game code. Lossy compression usually compresses more than lossless compression.

- Image file formats include PNG and SVG

- Audio file formats include ALAC, FLAC and WAV

- Video file formats include H.264 lossless and Motion JPEG Lossless

- Other file formats include ZIP for compressing files and folders.

An online service makes use of lossy compression when streaming films.

Give **one** advantage and **one** disadvantage of using lossy compression. [4]

Advantage: Smaller file sizes,[1] lower bandwidth (speed of Internet connection) required by the user.[1]

Disadvantage: Digital artefacts may be introduced by the compression[1] such as pixelation,[1] blurred edges,[1] and discolouration.[1]

PROPERTIES OF IMAGE FILES

When using image files, you must consider where it will be used as this will alter the technical requirements of the image. For instance, an image used in a printed magazine will need a very high resolution.

Resolution

Resolution is the number of pixels in a given area. It is measured as **dots per inch (DPI)** for print images and photographs and **pixels per inch (PPI)** for screen images.

The higher the DPI/PPI, the higher the image quality.

Printed documents such as books and posters typically use a resolution of 300 DPI. This means that there will be 300 printed dots in 1 inch (2.54 cm) of the printed document.

Web pages typically use images with a resolution of 72 DPI.

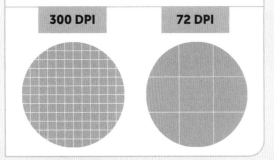

300 DPI   **72 DPI**

Pixel dimensions

This is the measurement of an image in pixels. It is calculated by multiplying the pixel width by the pixel height. In this example, the image measures 500 pixels wide and 300 pixels high so it has 15,000 pixels in total. A 10-megapixel camera will have 10 million pixels in one photo.

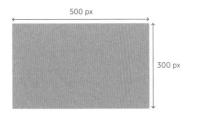

500 px

300 px

Static image file formats

JPG	Joint Photographic Experts Group

Compression: Lossy
Features: Very good compression. Works particularly well for photographs.
Uses: Photographs

PNG	Portable Network Graphics

Compression: Lossless
Features: Good compression. Allows for a transparent layer so a background can be seen behind.
Uses: Web images, particularly those that need transparency

SVG	Scalable Vector Graphics

Compression: Lossless
Features: Very small file size. Retains quality whatever size it is viewed at.
Uses: Web images, illustrations, cartoons

TIFF	Tagged Image File Format

Compression: No compression or lossless
Features: No data lost so very high quality files, but also large in size.
Uses: High quality printing

Vector images

Vector images are made up of shapes such as lines, curves and fills. Files are small in size and can be made bigger or smaller without affecting the quality of the image. They are commonly used for icons, logos, diagrams, animations and illustrations. SVG images are vector images.

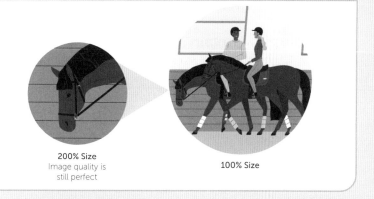

200% Size
Image quality is
still perfect

100% Size

Bitmap images

Bitmap images, also known as **raster images**, are made of small squares called pixels. File sizes tend to be larger. Images can be made smaller on the screen but if they are enlarged, they will become pixelated or blurry. Bitmap images are widely used in photographs. JPG, PNG and TIFF all use bitmap images.

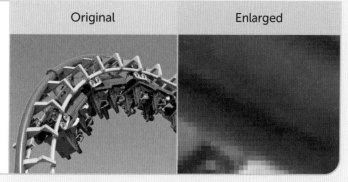

Original

Enlarged

A designer is creating a physical book called 'Relax'.

(a) State an appropriate DPI for the photographs contained in the book. [1]

(b) Identify an appropriate file format for the photographs. [1]

(c) The cover will feature an illustration of a person in a hammock. Explain why the illustrator might use a vector image format. [2]

(d) The book will be promoted on a website. State an appropriate PPI for a thumbnail image. [1]

(a) 300 DPI.[1]

(b) JPG / JPEG / PNG / TIFF.[1]

(c) Illustrations are made up of lines, curves and fills[1] so suitable to being created as a vector. By using a vector, the illustrator / graphic designer will be able to increase the size of the image without losing any quality.[1] It will also be easier to remove/edit parts of the images.[1]

(d) 72 PPI.[1]

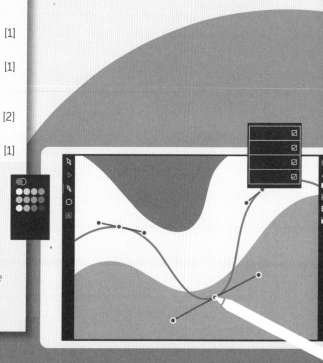

PROPERTIES OF AUDIO FILES

Audio files may contain music or spoken word such as audiobooks or radio.

Sample rate and bit depth

A sound wave is sampled many times per second. This is known as the **sample rate**. A sample is a measurement of the sound wave at a particular time. The accuracy of this measurement is known as the **bit depth**. The higher the sample rate and bit depth, the higher quality the sound will be.

CD quality sound uses a bit depth of 16 bits with a sample rate of 44.1 kilohertz (kHz). DVD and Blu-ray may use 16 bits or 24 bits. The sample rate is either 48 kHz or 96 kHz. This makes the sound quality used in films on DVD and Blu-ray better than CDs.

Audio file formats

MP3

Features: A lossy audio format with small file sizes around 10% the size of the original uncompressed files. They are widely used and can play on most devices. The name means MPEG-2 Audio Layer III.

Uses: Storing music on portable devices such as smartphones.

AAC

Features: A lossy format which has a higher sound quality than MP3 for the same bit rate and sample rate. AAC stands for Advanced Audio Coding.

Uses: The standard music format for iPhone®, iTunes®, PlayStation® and Android®.

FLAC

Features: A lossless compressed format. All the original data will be restored when the file is played. As it is a lossless format, it only compresses files to around 50-70% of their original size. FLAC stands for Free Lossless Audio Codec.

Uses: As there is no loss of quality it retains clarity of instruments and voices.

WAV

Features: This is a lossless, uncompressed format with no loss of audio quality.

Uses: Studio recordings.

Audio compression

Sound files may be **compressed**. When a lossy compression is used, listeners may notice some loss in sound quality.

Heavily compressed MP3 files, for instance, will lack depth and accuracy. CDs use **uncompressed** audio.

A band wants to record their latest single as a high-quality recording suitable for editing.

(a) Give an appropriate file format for the recording. [1]

(b) The band want to distribute their recording to fans. Explain your recommendation of a suitable format. [2]

(a) WAV,[1] FLAC[1]

(b) MP3 / AAC[1] as these are compressed formats which will require less storage space / require less bandwidth to stream.[1]

PROPERTIES OF MOVING IMAGE FILES

Moving image files include **video** and **animation**. Once any video editing is completed, the file will need to be exported to a video file format so it can be seen by the client or audience.

Rendering

When the file is exported, all visual effects and transitions are rendered by the computer. Rendering means the software processes all the editing data to make each frame of video.

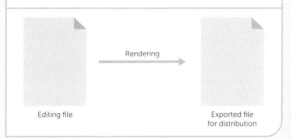

Editing file   Rendering   Exported file for distribution

SVG

As part of web pages, animation is usually stored in **SVG** format. This format allows objects to have motion and slide or bounce into position. This helps attract attention and is commonly seen with banner adverts. The format also allows the user to interact with the animation or image by moving the mouse or clicking.

GIF

GIF (Graphics Interchange Format) is an older format for animation on web pages. It has broadly been replaced by SVG.

Common video file formats

Animation video and film such as cartoons are distributed using ordinary video file formats.

MP4   MPEG-4 (Moving Picture Experts Group)

Features: Uses lossy compression to create a small file size. Works on a large number of devices.
Uses: A common format used for streaming video and films. Used in some Blu-rays.

AVI   Audio Video Interleave

Features: May be used for higher quality video.
Uses: The video may be compressed or uncompressed. It is therefore often suitable for professional high-quality video editing.

MPEG   MPEG-2

Features: Similar to MP4 but typically higher quality.
Uses: Used in television broadcasts, DVDs and some Blu-rays.

MOV   MOV

Features: A lossy compression format from Apple®.
Uses: This is the default recording format on Apple devices such as iPhone® and iPad® where it is very similar to MP4. MOV may contain different formats.

Screen resolution

The **resolution** of a screen is the total number of pixels it contains. It is usually given as the number of pixels in one row (width) and the number of pixels in one column (height). The more pixels that a screen has, the higher the quality of the image it displays.

High definition (HD) video has five times the number of pixels of **standard definition (SD)**. This results in clearer, more detailed images.

SD   Standard Definition

Resolution: 480p, 576p
Pixel dimensions: 640 × 480, 720 × 576
Use: Video sharing, broadcast TV and DVD.

HD   High Definition

Resolution: 1080p
Pixel dimensions: 1920 × 1080
Use: HD broadcast TV, Blu-ray.

4K UHD   Ultra High Definition

Resolution: 4K
Pixel dimensions: 3840 × 2160
Use: Cinema quality video, some Blu-ray discs and high-end gaming.

8K UHD   Ultra High Definition

Resolution: 8K
Pixel dimensions: 7690 × 4320
Use: Very high-end gaming and television. Feature films and visual effects may be shot at 8K.

Frame rate

The **frame rate** of a video is how quickly each image appears on the screen.

The standard frame rate for UK television is 25 frames per second (FPS). This means that 25 still images appear on the screen each second. Films often have a frame rate of 24 FPS. Higher frame rates are possible such as 60 FPS.

Higher frame rates lead to smoother motion. These are particularly common with computer games where they help players make split second decisions.

Most modern televisions and computer displays are capable of displaying video of 60 FPS or higher.	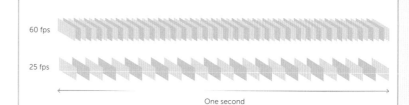
The cat jump shows 12 frames of animation. This would take 1 second at 12 FPS. It would take 0.4 seconds at 30 FPS.	

1. A natural history documentary will be distributed online and on Blu-ray in HD format.
   (a) State the meaning of the term HD. [1]
   The documentary will also be released as 4K UHD.
   (b) Explain the meaning of the term 4K UHD. [2]
   (c) Explain **one** benefit to the viewer in watching the 4K UHD version rather than the HD version. [2]

2. An action camera is used to record action in high-speed sports. The camera operates at 30, 60 or 120 FPS. Explain the advantage of using 120 FPS. [2]

1. (a) *High Definition.[1]*

   (b) *It is Ultra High Definition.[1] The pixel width is (just under) 4000 px.[1]*

   (c) *There will be more pixels shown on each frame[1] leading to more detail and crisper images.[1]*

2. *120 FPS will have four times the number of frames per second of 30 FPS.[1] This will result in smoother motion during any sports filmed.[1]*

EXAMINATION PRACTICE

> *Maya's Camping is a new campsite that has just opened. Maya, the owner would like to have some flyers produced as part of a marketing campaign.*
>
> *The flyer will have two versions. One version will be printed and posted to people on the mailing list for Maya's Camping. The second version will be uploaded to the website so visitors can download it. Each version will need to be an appropriate resolution.*

(a) Explain what is meant by 'resolution'. [2]

(b) Complete the sentences below choosing from the following options: [2]

| 25 | 30 | 60 | 72 | 300 |

A suitable dpi for the printed flyer would be _____ dpi

A suitable dpi for the online flyer would be _____ dpi

Maya has asked you to export the flyer so that it may be sent to the printers.

(c) Identify a suitable file format for exporting the flyer. [1]

(d) Maya would like the website version of the flyer to contain animation that reacts to the user hovering their mouse over it. Identify a suitable file format for the animation. [1]

As part of the marketing campaign, Maya's Camping have asked for a short promotional video to be made.

The video will be uploaded to their social media platforms and users will be able to stream the content on their smartphones or other internet enabled devices. Maya's Camping hope that the video will be widely shared.

(e) Explain **one** suitable file format for the video. [1]

(f) Explain what is meant by the term 'exporting' in this situation. [2]

(g) When exporting the video, one of the options given is frames per second. Explain why selecting 2 FPS would not be suitable. [2]

Maya has also asked for a radio advert to be produced.

The recording company has said that they will record the advert using a high bit rate of 24-bits and a high sample rate of 192 kHz. They will save the advert using a file format that makes use of lossless compression.

(h) Explain what is meant by sample rate. [2]

(i) Describe how the sound quality would differ if the recording company made use of a lossy compression file format. [2]

TOPICS FOR THE ASSESSMENT
R094 Visual identity and digital graphics

Information about this mandatory unit

Non examined assessment (NEA)
Duration 10–12 hours
50 marks
25% of the qualification

Specification coverage

Knowledge of visual identity and digital graphics, topic areas 1–3.

Topic Area 1: Develop visual identity
Topic Area 2: Plan digital graphics for products
Topic Area 3: Create visual identity and digital graphics

Tasks

Task 1: Design a visual identity, including a logo, appropriate for the audience and intended purpose. Justify how and why the visual identity meets the client's needs. Record details of any assets that will be used in an assets table. Create appropriate planning documents such as a workplan, mind map, mood board and visualisation diagram.

Task 2: Create graphical assets and save them with a suitable format, dimensions and resolution. Create the digital graphic using image editing software. Make effective use of tools, techniques and design concepts demonstrating how the graphic meets the client's needs. Export the graphic in two appropriate formats.

THE TASKS

This unit expects you to produce both a **visual identity** and **digital graphics** that make use of the identity.

A visual identity helps to give viewers the values and core principles of a product, service, company or organisation. It helps with brand recognition and is used in marketing to a target audience.

The digital graphic product that you make should be created using specialist graphics editing software such as Adobe® Photoshop®, Serif® Affinity® Photo or GIMP.

You will be given a **project brief** to read. This will cover all the requirements you need to meet.

There will then be **two** tasks.

Task 1 (20 marks)	Design a visual identity (6 marks)	You will need to design the component features of the visual identity, including: • Logo* • Name • Slogan or strap line	The following elements of a visual identity should be shown: • Graphic style including shapes and symbols • Typography • Colour palette and meaning • Layout and complexity
	Justify your design choices (8 marks)	You need to justify your design choices. You will do this using: • A report* • Annotation	
	Produce relevant planning documents and identify assets to be used (6 marks)	It is up to you which **planning documentation** you decide to use. It is likely, though, that you will produce the following: • Mind map • Mood board • Concept sketch • Visualisation diagram* Identify the assets that will be used or created. These should be listed along with details, sources and permissions in: • An asset table*	

Task 2 (30 marks)	Create the visual identity (6 marks)
	Create other assets for the graphic product (6 marks)
	Create the graphic product (12 marks)
	Export the graphic product (6 marks)

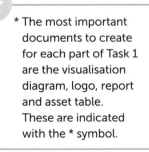

* The most important documents to create for each part of Task 1 are the visualisation diagram, logo, report and asset table. These are indicated with the * symbol.

PURPOSE OF A VISUAL IDENTITY

A **visual identity** gives customers or users a feeling and perception of the brand, product or service. It helps to visually communicate the values and personality of the brand with audiences or customers.

Brands with a strong visual identity have an emotional connection with users and customers. The visual identity helps to **establish a brand**, make it stand out and develop **brand loyalty** over time.

A strong visual or brand identity is important to help customers recognise the brand. A brand's visual identity, including logos, colours, fonts and tone of voice, will be used throughout all of a brand's media products, from their company letterhead to their billboard poster or website. Companies usually have a set of **brand guidelines** to achieve this. Consistent use of this **house style** creates familiarity and ensures that the audience or customer recognises and remembers a brand.

All brands try to create a visual identity. Think about the latest product you bought, a restaurant you ate in or an advert you saw. What feelings and brand image did it give you? Why did it make you think this way?

Before you begin

As you develop your product's visual identity, you will need to **justify** your design choices. Justifying means that you have fully explained your reasons for doing something.

You may do this by **annotating** designs and/or producing a **report**.

An advantage of creating a report is that all your evidence will be in one place.

It's a good idea to make a report at the start of the project so that you have somewhere to put everything.

VISUAL IDENTITY DESIGN STYLE

Business type and brand values

A visual identity design style should reflect the type of business or organisation that it represents. It should help to **communicate the values** and core principles of the brand.

For instance, Kids Zone offer holiday clubs to young children. They wanted to create a visual identity that communicated feelings of fun, activity and creativity. They made use of bright colours as these would be attractive and appealing to children. The typeface chosen uses a playful decorative font. By using pencil sketches behind the logo they helped to create a playful and active perception.

By contrast, Royal Swan wanted a visual identity that showed an elegant and refined hotel.

They made use of a gold colour on the swan to suggest luxury. A contrasting dark blue colour was chosen to help give reassurance and trust in the brand. The chosen logo uses simple lines to help give a feeling of a clean, elegant design that is memorable. The choice of a serif typeface for the title helps to communicate a traditional atmosphere, whilst the use of a sans-serif typeface for the strap line 'Boutique Hotel' suggests a modern twist.

Brand positioning

The **brand's position** in the marketplace can also be reflected in the visual identity design style.

The style will change depending on whether a brand positions itself as an **economy**, **mid-range** or **luxury brand**.

Notice the visual identity of a brand of baked beans in a supermarket. A standard font, simple graphics and white background all help to give the feeling of an economy brand.

By contrast, a luxury brand of beans may have a stylish label that has been beautifully designed along with a highly crafted image of the beans.

COMPONENTS OF VISUAL IDENTITY

Branding

The following are the components that you need to consider when creating a visual identity:

- **Logo** – word(s) and/or images to represent the brand
- **Brand name**
- **Slogan** or **Strapline** – a short memorable phrase

Before developing your visual identity, you may like to create a mind map. See **page 86 & 87** for more details and examples.

You will need to produce a logo to obtain marks for your visual identity in Task 1.

Note

When creating your visual identity, you will just be asked to 'Design a visual identity'.

You need to decide which parts of visual identity are required for the product you have been asked to make.

Areas you should consider include:

- Logo
- Name
- Slogan/strap line
- Graphical style
- Typography
- Colour palette
- Layout

You will need to show evidence for this in your planning documents such as mood boards, concept sketches, mind maps and visualisation diagrams.
Your report will also allow you to record any justifications or decisions.

Elements of visual identity

The following elements help to create a visual identity:

Typography

The style of the text used.

Graphics

This includes photos, images, illustrations, **shapes** and **symbols**.

Colour palette

The particular group of colours or colour scheme that is to be used across all products.

Layout and complexity

Layouts may be simple or complex. You will need to consider the audience and purpose of the product to decide which is appropriate.

MOOD BOARD

Mood boards

A **mood board** is a collection of images, text and colours that generate ideas for the look and feel of a product. They can be digital, (created on a computer), or physical.

A mood board is unlikely to include images used in the final product, but instead is there to give an idea for the theme, based on the client brief.

A mood board is a key part of the planning process and should be created when planning the visual identity for the graphic product.

Example of a physical mood board

Creating a mood board

When gathering content for the mood board, aim for a good variety of images, text that illustrates the typography and colours that will give a clear idea of the intended colour palette for the visual identity and digital graphic.

When creating your mood board, use all available space and fill the page. If creating a digital mood board, Photoshop, Affinity® Photo, Word and PowerPoint are all examples of appropriate software for achieving this.

A physical mood board may also contain examples of textures and fabrics. A digital mood board may contain photos of these.

If you produce a physical mood board, you will need to take a photo of it or scan it to submit to the exam board.

Example of a digital mood board

 If appropriate, make a mood board for your project brief.

 A mood board will probably be the first planning document you create as it helps to give a feel for the visual identity of all other planning documents you will make

Include graphics and photos that give a feel for the visual identity, not ones that you will use in the final product.

For more information about mood boards see **page 37**.

CONCEPT SKETCH

A **concept sketch** is a series of simple freehand drawings or sketches that are used to develop an idea. This may also include some annotations with brief explanations of colour or the design itself.

Concepts sketches are a good way to get basic ideas down on paper. As multiple ideas are created side by side, it is also a good way to compare and consider different potential ideas and select those that can be developed further.

Features of a concept sketch

- Sketches are brief, usually just outlining the ideas.
- These give the feel of the idea rather than any detailed response to the brief.
- Commonly drawn in pencil or pen to quickly create multiple concepts.

 If appropriate, make concept sketches for your logo and other elements of your visualisation diagram.

Example of a concept sketch for a logo design

FAQs

When do you need to use a concept sketch?

A concept sketch is great for showing how you have developed elements of the identity or final graphic. For instance, you may create a concept sketch to show how you developed a logo. All these sketches should be photographed or scanned and added to your report or evidence folder.

You may create concept sketches to show the development of your ideas for your visualisation diagram.

BIG TREE CAMPING

Example client brief

Big Tree Camping offers unique camping experiences for young adults and families who are looking for a break that takes them truly back to nature. Big Tree Camping offers an authentic, budget friendly alternative for those who really want to get away from it all.

They are relaunching their brand and have asked for a visual identity that reflects their values and appeals to the target audience. Big Tree Camping are already adopting energy efficiency and only use sustainable materials. They believe in taking care of the environment. This needs to be reflected in the design.

Logo and name

A central element of the visual identity for a brand is the logo.

Below shows an example of how a student has made use of concept sketches to develop a logo design.

Concept sketches for logo design

Chosen logo: 4

I wanted to give the feeling of a hot summer's day so decided to add a sun behind the tent and trees.

This logo will work in black and white or in colour. It will also work in various sizes given its simple design. Only the sun should be coloured so that the logo design has more impact.

The tent and tree symbols show that the campsite is in a natural setting in the woods. This fits well with the client brief which tries to suggest how they will be getting 'truly back to nature'. The tree symbols also link with the idea of taking care of the environment which was a key part of the client brief.

 When designing your logo, refer back to the client brief and make sure your design reflects the identity they were looking for.

Slogan or strap line

The slogan should be short and snappy. You may like to suggest some ideas and settle on a final slogan or strap line.

Slogan:
Big tree, big adventure

Colour palette and meaning

The colours selected should be a good fit for the brand and target audience, helping to communicate the key messages you want to get across. Remember that colours help to give different feelings and meanings, so they should be carefully considered.

Here is an example of an approach to the **Big Tree Camping** brief.

Colour scheme

When choosing a colour scheme for Big Tree Camping, I felt that earthy colours would be most suitable. Browns and greens would help to suggest forests and woodland. They would also help get across the environmentally sustainable nature of the camp site.

The yellow is bright and will work well in the logo to attract attention and be appealing to young children. It will help to give a fresh and vibrant image.

| #F08D1E | #81623F | #406D35 | #FEE31B |

Colour schemes are the colours that have been chosen to be used in products. The following sites will help you to design colour schemes that use harmonious or complementary colours that work well together:

- https://paletton.com/
- https://color.adobe.com/
- https://colordesigner.io/

Be precise with your choice of colours by using the hex code or RGB values to specify your colour choice.

Colour codes typically use numbers from 0–255 for red, green and blue. Hex codes typically use numbers from 00 to FF. FF is the equivalent of 255 in decimal numbers.

For more information about colour see **page 15**.

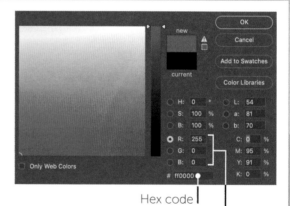

Hex code

RGB values

Typography

Typography is the style of text and is made up of the typeface (font style), font size and the arrangement of the text on the page, such as line spacing.

It is important that the choice of font reflects the message that you want to give the target audience. For instance, a serif font may be used for a more traditional feel.

Typography

My mood board looked at some ideas for typography in the visual identity. I wanted to give a wooden, earthy feel to the text and feel that having the text filled with wood grain would help with this. The vintage feel of the 'RUST' typeface, with a serif font, seems a little too traditional. I think that the 'CABIN' typeface gives a natural feel that looks like it has been etched into the wood and would be appealing to children and young families.

I have chosen 'Modern Grunge' as the font for the logo and titles.

BIG TREE CAMPING

I then want to use a simpler sans-serif font for the main text as this will be easier to read. I have chosen to use Arial...

Part of the moodboard showing typography

Design each of the following that are appropriate for your project brief:
- Logo
- Name
- Strapline / slogan
- Colour palette
- Typography

Remember to justify your choices in your report and/or using annotation.

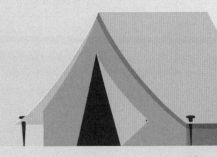

CONCEPTS OF GRAPHIC DESIGN

Graphic design concepts

You should consider the key concepts of graphic design before you plan your final product, including:

Application of visual identity	Typography
Alignment	Use of white space
Use of colour and colour systems	

Colour systems

Colours are represented in graphic design using a number of different systems. When setting up a graphic you should choose the most appropriate setting.

Graphic design example

This example shows a final page spread (two pages) from a recipe book. Read the annotations and consider how various concepts of graphic design have been used.

White space is the area that is purposefully left blank around objects. Here lots of white space has been left around the title to help it stand out.

A sans serif typeface has been used to make the title stand out and have a modern, fresh feel.

The ingredients and method are both aligned to the top of their text boxes.

A serif font has been used on the text, as this makes it easier to read when printed.

Additional white space has been kept in the page so that it doesn't feel cluttered. It also allows longer recipes to be used.

The orange colour used is consistent in both the text at the top and the shape fill colour.

CMYK colours will be used.

The title, serving size, ingredients, cooking time and page number are all left-aligned to a guide line.

Macaroni Cheese

Serves 2

150g macaroni

30g butter

25g plain flour

500ml milk

150g Cheddar cheese (grated)

1. Melt the butter into a pan and heat until foaming.
2. Stir in the flour slowly.
3. Cook together for two minutes.
4. Slowly stir in the milk.
5. Add the macaroni.
6. Cover and cook for 15 minutes, stirring occasionall
7. Add the cheese and stir in.

20 mins

Tips

Remember to cook the butter and flour together for at least two minutes to avoid a floury taste in the macaroni cheese.

Calories 470 | Fat 27g | Protein 17g | Fibre 2g
Carbohydrates 42g | Sodium 0.7g

16

Nutritional information is aligned centrally.

Colour trends

Pantone®

Pantone is a system that allows colours to be precisely matched. For instance, one spot colour on a logo may be specified with a Pantone colour.

NCS (Natural Colour System®)

This system allows colours to be specified using the way colours are perceived.

Colour modes

RGB

Red, green, blue.
This corresponds to the pixels on a screen. It is used for television and web images.

CMYK

Cyan, magenta, yellow, key (black).
Each colour corresponds to the ink colour used in the print process. This is used in print products such as books, magazines and posters.

The recipe book has simple recipes. The photography therefore presents each dish in a simple way. The style of the photography will be the same for all photos in the book and in line with the visual identity.

Photos would use CMYK in a printed book and RGB for any images used online.

The right page number and chapter title are right-aligned

Easy dishes | 17

LAYOUT CONVENTIONS FOR DIFFERENT GRAPHIC PRODUCTS AND PURPOSES

In the assessment, you will be asked to make one graphical product. You will need to consider the layout conventions for the particular product that you have been asked to make. Layout conventions include where graphics and text are typically located and the dimensions of the product. The following pages show some key conventions to consider for each type of product.

Print advertisement

Print advertisements are found in magazines or newspapers and are used to raise awareness of a product as well as to persuade people to buy a product or service.

Typical conventions:

Graphics related to the product or service

The style of these graphics will depend on the audience and purpose. For example, an advert for a fast-food chain might include visually appealing images of the food available. By contrast, an advert for a toy shop might include cartoon style images to appeal to a younger audience.

Catchy slogan or tagline

A successful advert usually contains a slogan or tagline. This is often a memorable phrase or a rhetorical question that helps viewers remember the advert or encourages them to take an action.

Logo and/or company name

The company or brand of the product or service must be obvious. This is usually communicated through the logo and name. Expect to see the use of the brand's **house style** in the colour and fonts that are used.

Clear, concise text

Messaging in advertising should be clear and to the point so it is quickly understood by the viewer.

Example

The box opposite shows a clear **call to action** asking customers to visit the website by clicking the banner advert. This advert has used large bold text to create impact in the **title**. The bright colours in the **images** attract attention and link to the word 'Spring'. The use of red on the 50% circle suggests a sticker and attracts the eye to the discount.

Additional information is kept small so as not to distract from the main message.

CD, DVD, Blu-Ray covers

Disc box covers aim to attract customers to purchase the film, music or game. They should give a feeling of the genre and often make use of a photo of key characters.

Typical conventions:

Images relevant to the content

Images will be chosen to appeal to the audience. For DVD and Blu-Ray covers, the aim is normally to persuade potential customers that this is a film or series that they would want to watch. For CDs, the purpose of the cover may be to attract attention. Equally, as many fans may treasure the physical item, images which enhance or promote the musician's values may be used.

Additional information

On DVDs and Blu-ray the additional information will include a description of the film. Whilst key actors and the director may appear on the front cover, most cast and crew appear in a very small font size on the back cover. For CDs, additional information is placed on the back and includes the track listing, play times and copyright information.

Clear, bold title

The title should appear on both the front and the spine of the case. This means however it is displayed, the title is visible. Titles are typically placed at the top or bottom of the front cover.

Legal information – the 'small print'

This is usually found on the back of the product and includes details such as the copyright information for the product. For DVDs and Blu-ray, BBFC age ratings symbols will also be used.

Example

- CD front insert: 120mm (w) × 120mm (h)
- CD back insert: 151mm (w) × 118mm (h)
- DVD cover: 184mm (w) × 274mm (h)
            (14mm spine)
- Blu-Ray cover: 148mm (w) × 272mm (h)
            (14mm spine)

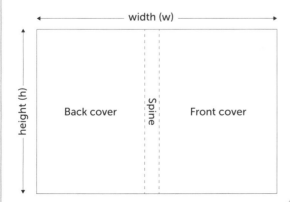

If you are asked to produce a CD, DVD or Blu-Ray cover, read the project brief carefully. If you are given dimensions, you must use the ones in the project brief.

Posters

Printed posters are used to advertise or promote a product service or to inform and educate. It is important that their design is simple and eye catching. Advertising posters aim to attract customers to a business or to sell products. Posters have a variety of sizes for different uses. Both portrait and landscape orientations may be used.

Typical conventions:

A logo and/or company name

This should be clearly visible, using the font style and colours of the brand so that it is quickly recognised.

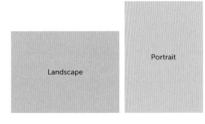

A key message

Most posters, especially those in advertising, will have a key message. This should be short and to the point as people may have only a few seconds to read the poster. White space is also important to allow the message to be clearly seen. Take into account the details of the project brief. If the poster is to be displayed in schools and to promote exercise for school children, they may have longer to read the information whilst they wait for a class to start. This would allow more information to be added.

A logo and/or company name

Images should not only be relevant but also support the message being delivered. If you are advertising a new smartphone, for example, an image of the smartphone should make it look appealing and a desirable product. Remember it is okay to highlight the most important part of an image and crop the remainder. For instance, a poster for a car advert could use just the headlights and wing mirror of the car to show a sleek refined look.

Examples

The key message in this poster is the 50% off sale. The photo and model chosen support the idea of a smart casual brand. The logo in the bottom right helps the viewer to know which shop to purchase the item from.

The typography of the Jazz Festival poster matches the flowing graphics that have been used. This helps to give a fun and party feeling to the event. Again, the logo is present. The name of the festival and date use large text, whilst less important information uses a small font size.

Leaflets

A leaflet is a printed graphic used to promote a product or service.

Typical conventions:

| **The logo for the company** |
| **Copy is written in paragraphs** |

| **A clear title on the front cover** | **Relevant images illustrate the copy** |

| **Clear titles are given for pages or sections** |

Leaflet folds

Consider carefully how leaflets fold. It is a good idea to fold a blank piece of paper, then label each section before you set up your page in graphics editing software.

An example of a tri-fold (three fold) leaflet is shown, but bi-fold (two fold) leaflets are also very common.

| Page 2 | Back | Front | | Page 1 | Page 3 | Page 4 |

Example

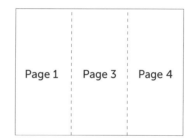

HydroChill is a company that makes an innovative new system for keeping water bottles cold all day. Their tri-fold leaflet maintains typical conventions such as a logo and title on the front page.

Typography is simple and modern helping to show a contemporary brand. Images help to give the feel of a refreshing way to hydrate. Colours have been kept consistent throughout the leaflet.

If you are asked to produce a leaflet, check the project brief very carefully for any folds required and the dimensions of the page that will be folded.

Magazine cover

Magazine covers are designed to appeal to their target audience. The style and layout should help to entice people to want to buy and read the magazine.

Typically, a title is given at the top of the magazine. The image used will be one of the most important features as it will attract attention. Don't forget additional conventions such as the use of a barcode, issue number, date and price.

Titles are typically at the top of a magazine. Other important information is also contained at the top, such as the issue number and date. Together these make up the **masthead**.

Typography is very important in magazines. Here, a grunge font style has been chosen to help fit with the image of skateboarding.

Top 10 UK skate spots | Quick fix repairs

DARK SLIDE

for skaters by skaters

issue 37 | 29 Sept

getting
GNARLY
with ZÖE

Learn **NEW** tricks
Meet US Champ
Shane Huston

£3.99

LATEST NEWS:
World Skateboarding Championships

Additional information such as the **price** and **barcode** are important features of a magazine.

Typically, the price will be in a small font size, however, for cheaper magazines it may be a selling feature and be presented in a shape, to look like a sticker, for more impact.

Magazines typically have one **image** that fills the cover. Typically, the image relates to the main story in the magazine. The aim of this photograph or graphic is to attract people to pick up and buy the magazine. It should give a feel that meets the visual identity of the magazine issues.

Cover lines are titles and snippets from stories that are featured. They should entice readers without giving away the full story.

Book cover

Book covers tend to contain less information on the cover than magazines. The dimensions are usually smaller too, especially for novels. Book covers use one sheet of paper for the front, back and spine. Be careful to check the client brief to see exactly what dimensions are required and which parts of the book cover you have been asked to make.

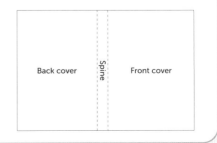

Back cover | Spine | Front cover

Book cover typical conventions

Spine

The spine is the part of the book that shows if it is on a bookcase. It tends to have the title and author name along with the publisher's logo. As it is very thin, it tends to have few if any graphics, however, it is likely to use the background colour of the front and back covers.

Back cover

The back cover will contain an overview of the book. For novels, the copy should entice the reader into the plot of the story, whilst leaving them interested in what happens next. The back cover will contain additional information such as the barcode and price.

The book title and author

This is key information for the audience and should be positioned prominently. White space around these elements help make them stand out. The font size used for the name of the author will depend on how important they are in helping to sell the book. A book with an established best-selling author may have their name even larger than the book title. However, in most books, the name will use a relatively small font size.

Relevant images giving hints of the book's contents.

The choice of image is made carefully to help show the genre of book along with some aspect of the story. Photographs or illustrations are frequently used. A lot of time will be spent choosing or editing images as these are highly important in attracting buyers.

Examples

'The new life' makes use of simple illustration to give a quirky and perhaps humorous feel to the cover. The typography for the title helps to give a playful feel.

'Discovered' makes use of an ancient house in fog to create an eerie feel suggesting a horror or murder mystery.
A serif font has been chosen to give a more traditional feel.

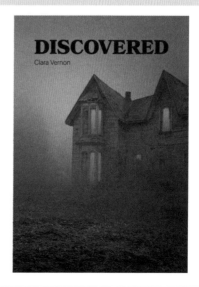

OTHER LAYOUT CONVENTIONS

Packaging

Product packaging design is used to make a product stand out on shelf. It often includes important information too.

Typical conventions:

Logo and company name.

A barcode and sometimes a price.

The name of the product.

Relevant graphics, for example images of the product.

Information about how to use the product or what it contains such as nutritional information on a cereal packet.

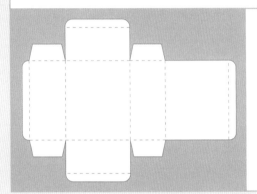

Packaging often uses complicated layouts, known as nets, which fold into a 3D shape. As with leaflets, it will be useful to design the layout first on paper.

Multimedia products

Multimedia products include websites, apps and kiosks. The features of these products will vary depending on the type of product.

Typical conventions:

Logo and/or company name.

Navigational features such as buttons, hyperlinks, drop downs and rollovers.

Relevant multimedia content such as images, photos, videos, animations or sounds.

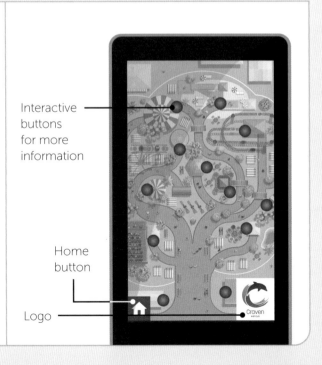

Interactive buttons for more information

Home button

Logo

Web images and graphics

Images and graphics are extensively used on websites. Uses vary widely from banner adverts and photographs that illustrate products to individual graphics for buttons.

Multiple users may update different sections of a website. For example, a web designer may create the structure and template graphics, whilst a photographer may create individual photos. A content management system may be used to combine all these assets into the web page.

Typical conventions:

Graphics on websites will have precise pixel dimensions so they correctly fit into the design.

All images and graphics will need to fit with the visual identity of the brand – for example, the colour scheme.

Logos and the website name are likely to feature prominently to help users identify that they are on the correct website.

Examples

Banner ads

Certain areas of a web page may be used to display banner ads.

These will need to be exact dimensions.

Banner ads typically have little text and a key action inside a button, e.g. "BOOK NOW". Animation may be used to attract attention.

Web images

Web images may need to be created as assets for each object, such as a button or radio button, on a web page.

Button states, such as up, down and hover, may need to be created.

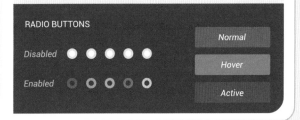

Game layouts

Game layouts will vary depending on the type of game. However, all games include a graphical user interface with features such as buttons, hyperlinks or drop-down menus.

The style of graphics and a colour palette needs to match the needs of the audience and the type of game that has been made.

Example

'Bubble Trouble Shooter' makes use of bright colours that are appealing to young people, but also emphasise the casual gaming audience. A clear 'play' button is easy to find on the screen. Other buttons make use of icons to help keep the menu screen simple. The graphics give a good feel for the type of game that is about to begin. Red circles have been used to attract attention to notifications on certain icons.

MIND MAP

A mind map is a document that is used to help generate ideas.

Be creative in the ideas you come up with. Remember, your ideas will evolve as you plan, design and create your final product. You certainly aren't fixed to the ideas you give on an early mind map.

A mind map created at the start of developing a visual identity for a new restaurant

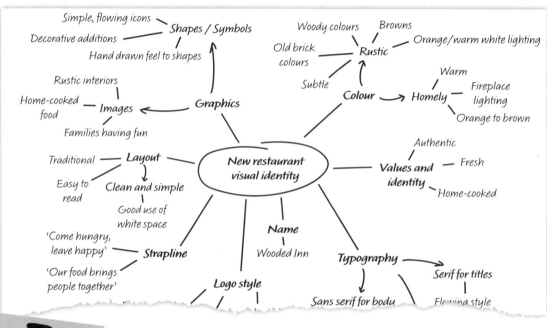
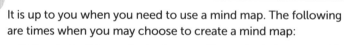

It is up to you when you need to use a mind map. The following are times when you may choose to create a mind map:

- At the start of the project when working out what you need to do from the brief.
- To spark ideas for the visual identity, such as colours, logo ideas, and types of emotion you are trying to create.
- To plan all the components that may be required in a visualisation diagram.

Mind maps should be produced quickly. Don't worry about mistakes – the purpose is to spark ideas. You may find that a good hand-drawn mind map is possible to make in just 10 minutes. Photograph it and add it to your report.

Whilst you are allowed to make a digital mind map on a computer, you may find that this restricts your creativity and wastes time.

For more information about mind maps, see **page 36**.

CRITTER ADVENTURES

Example client brief

Critter Adventures offers hands on animal experiences at schools and children's birthday parties in the local area. During their animal handling sessions, children aged 5-11 can get up close to creatures such as insects, lizards, snakes and even a tarantula! It is both entertaining and educational, with information about how to care for these animals playing a key part of the sessions.

Critter Adventures are looking to increase their birthday party bookings. They have asked you to design a half page magazine advert that will appear in a local magazine aimed at families. It should include key information about the parties, as well as how to get in touch for booking.

The dimensions of the advert will be 210 mm × 148 mm.

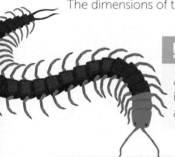

> **! Note**
>
> Assume at this point that a visual identity including logo, name and slogan have already been created.

Designing the product

Mind map

First a mind map was created to plan what is required on the visualisation diagram.

This book shows examples of mind maps made for the visual identity and graphical product. It is up to you to decide when a mind map would be an appropriate planning tool to use in your assessment. You may make more than one if this helps you.

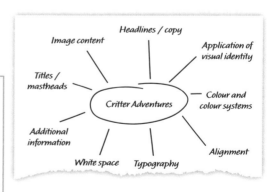

Concept sketches

Concept sketches may be used to develop ideas before creating your final visualisation diagram. These will have less detail, and be faster to produce, than the visualisation diagram itself.

Page 72 describes how concept sketches could be used to create a logo.

The following shows concept sketches for the development of ideas for the Critter Adventures advert.

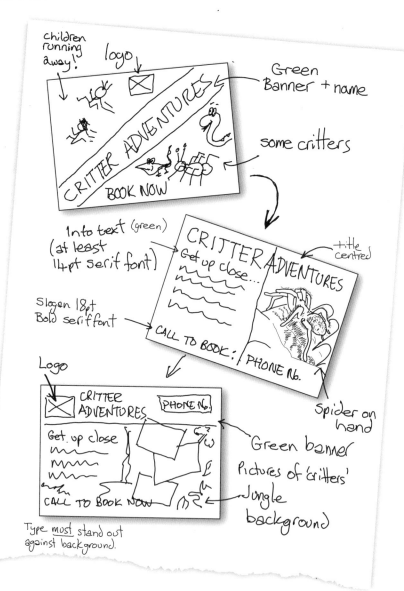

Concept sketches allow you to be creative and quickly come up with ideas for your final product. You may use them to develop the whole product, or different parts of the product.

You shouldn't spend long developing each concept sketch. Remember their purpose is to come up with ideas.

Take photographs of any concept sketches you produce then add them to your report along with any annotation.

Be careful not to throw away sketches and ideas. These will be useful evidence of your product planning and development.

For more information on concept sketches, see **pages 71 & 72**.

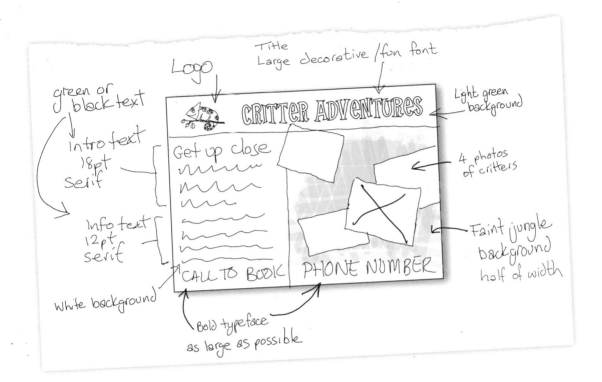

Annotations on the visualisation diagram:

- Logo
- Title — Large decorative / fun font
- green or black text
- intro text 18pt serif
- Info text 12pt serif
- White background
- Bold typeface as large as possible
- Light green background
- 4 photos of critters
- Faint jungle background half of width

Sketch text: CRITTER ADVENTURES · Get up close · CALL TO BOOK · PHONE NUMBER

 Create and design each of the following that are appropriate for your project brief:

- Mind map
- Concept sketch
- Visualisation diagram

Remember to justify your choices in your report and/or using annotation.

Developing a visualisation diagram on paper with a sketch will probably be easier to create. Once complete, just take a photograph of it and add it to your report.

You may choose to then make annotations by hand or using software. See pages 42-43 for more information.

TECHNICAL PROPERTIES OF GRAPHICS

Bitmap images

Bitmap images are made up of small blocks called pixels, from the words 'picture elements'. There are a number of technical properties that you need to be aware of before you source or create any assets for your final graphical product.

Colour depth

Colour depth is the number of colours that are available to represent each channel (red, green or blue) for each pixel. For most images, 8-bit colour is a good choice.

Colour depth: 8-bit
Available colours:
16.8 million colours

Colour depth: 4-bit
Available colours:
4096 colours

Colour depth: 2-bit
Available colours:
64 colours

Colour mode

When editing images, you need to choose a **colour mode**, either RGB or CMYK.

For digital products, the RGB (red, green, blue) colour mode should be selected. This corresponds with the red, green and blue light that makes up each pixel.

Cyan, magenta, yellow and black (CMYK) are the colours used in the printing process. Each dot of ink or toner in an image is made from these four colours.

Compression settings and overall quality

Certain formats such as JPG allow you to change the **quality settings**. Lower quality leads to a lower image size, but a poorer image. Typically, you should select a good quality or higher. PNG images aren't compressed, so there is no loss of quality when saving or exporting.

Good compression quality

File format and size:
JPG, 151 kB

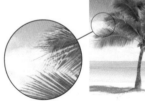

Very poor compression quality

File format and size:
JPG, 5.3 kB

Transparency

Areas of bitmap images may be made transparent. This is usually shown as a grey and white checkerboard. Any areas that are transparent will allow a background lower layer to be seen.

Image placed over green background or layer

If you need your assets to have **transparency**, PNG should be used as it supports a transparency layer known as an alpha channel.

Vector graphics

Vector graphics are built using shapes, lines, strokes and fills. They have **scalability**, which means that increasing the image size doesn't affect the quality of the image. Most logos and illustrations are usually best created using vector graphics.

The **file size** of vector graphics is usually smaller than the equivalent bitmap image. However, most vector image formats require specialist **software support** to open, edit or view them. Vector graphics may be suitable formats for assets, however, a final digital graphic will need to be in an appropriate **compatible** format for users to view or print.

Software that is suitable for creating vector graphics includes Adobe® Illustrator, Affinity® Designer and Inkscape. If you are making images for a website, most web browsers support SVG. For print products, EPS (Encapsulated PostScript) is generally used. For most digital products, if a vector graphic is used as an asset, it will need to be exported as a PNG before it is printed or shown on a display.

For more information on bitmap and vector graphics, see **page 59**.

The designers of Hawthorn Dental Care's logo made use of a vector graphic. Whatever size the logo is, it will always appear sharp and of high quality.

They have provided the dental practice with both a PNG and SVG version of the graphic which can be used in stationery, appointment cards, posters and their website.

SOURCING ASSETS

Before you make your final digital graphic, you will need to source suitable assets. This may include logos, illustrations, graphics and photographs.

When sourcing images you need to be aware of the licences that they contain and any permissions that would need to be obtained.

Where to source assets from

Client images

The client may provide assets such as a logo or photographs for your use. Even though the client has supplied the images, care must be taken using them as they may still have rights and permissions associated with them. For instance, a photograph that a client used in a previous advertising billboard may not have permission from the model or photographer to use it in other publications. **Logos** may have very strict rules on how they are allowed to be used.

The Internet

The Internet is a valuable resource when finding assets to use in a graphic product. When using **search engines**, make use of search engine **filters** to narrow down the image size, colours used, type of image and any permissions or licence that the image has. Remember that personal images and those shared on social media are also likely to have limitations in whether they are allowed to be used. Always check permissions before using.

Photographs

A photographer might be commissioned to take specific **photographs** to be used as assets in the final digital graphic. Whilst you will not be able to commission a photographer in your assessment, you may choose to take your own photographs to use as assets in your final graphical product.

When you source assets for this project, you are not expected to obtain licences, seek permission to use an image or make any payment of fees.

You may still use the images in your assessment, however, you must make it clear in the 'permissions' section of your assets table as to what legal permissions you would need or licence type you would select.

Stock libraries

A number of **stock libraries** are available for use by media companies and professionals. These have high-quality images (stock) which may be chosen by designers for use in their media projects. When using a stock library, users can search through thousands of low-resolution images that contain watermarks. These may be downloaded to see how the image works in their graphic design. Once they have decided on the images they would like to use, the licence and fee is agreed and then a high-resolution image, without a watermark is made available for downloading.

Stock libraries include Shutterstock, Alamy and Getty Images. There are also a variety of image libraries with assets protected by Creative Commons licences such as www.pixabay.com, www.unsplash.com and www.pexels.com.

Be careful to record any permissions or restrictions that are associated with each image that you use from a stock library.

Once you have a plan for how your digital graphic could look, you need to find suitable assets and note their details, including permission for use. You can use either the OCR-provided template or create your own. You must reference any template you use, even if it is the OCR-provided one.

Here is an example of how this could be approached:

Example

Asset table

Asset	Properties	Source	Legal issues	Use
Logo.svg	Full colour vector	I made this	None	Visual identity
Lizard.jpg	3988 × 3988px 96 DPI	https://en.wikipedia.org/wiki/Lizard	Creative Commons Attribution-Share Alike 4.0 International license. Need to give credit to the author.	To show the animals at parties.
Grass.jpg	2048 × 2048	https://media.gettyimages.com/photos/grass-picture-id494331215	For my final graphic, I would need to buy the large version. This has a fee of £375. Royalty-free so no conditions on usage.	Background image.

Once you have a plan for how your digital graphic should look, you need to find suitable assets and note their details, including permissions for use. You can use either the OCR-provided template or your own. If you use a template it must be referenced.

For more information on assets logs, see **page 45**.

Stage	Task	Completed
Report	Create a report which justifications and evidence are added to.	☐
	Read the client brief carefully.	☐
	Consider the target audience and mood needed for the final product.	☐
	Create a mind map of key parts of the client brief.	☐
Design a visual identity	Create a mood board for the visual identity that you will create.	☐
	Create concept sketches of a logo and...	☐
	...justify your design decisions using annotations and/or your report.	☐
	Create other elements that will make up the visual identity. Justify your design choices in your annotation and/or report.	☐
	Create a mind map of key aspects of the visualisation diagram you are about to produce.	☐
	Create concept sketches of the layout and...	☐
	...justify your design decisions using annotations and/or your report.	☐
Plan the digital graphic product	Create a visualisation diagram to clearly show how the graphic will look, including annotations to show colours, fonts and graphics that would be used and...	☐
	...justify your design decisions that haven't already been justified in annotations in your report.	☐
	Record the details of any assets to be used in the final graphic, including the details of each of their permissions, in an assets table.	☐

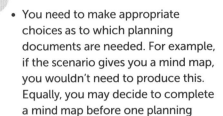

- You need to make appropriate choices as to which planning documents are needed. For example, if the scenario gives you a mind map, you wouldn't need to produce this. Equally, you may decide to complete a mind map before one planning stage, but not another.

- It is your decision as to which elements you will design for the visual identity, but you must include a logo as one of the elements.

- A successful visualisation diagram should be detailed enough that a designer could use it to create the final product. Hand drawn sketches with detailed annotation is a good choice.

- Asset tables need to be detailed including specific details on any legal issues. Remember, you are designing for commercial use, not for personal or educational use.

- The project brief you are given will contain a copy of the mark scheme. Check this carefully to see how marks are awarded for each section.

Evidence

Evidence you should have in files or your report:
- Report – containing justifications
- Mind map(s)
- Mood board
- Concept sketches
- Logo design
- Other elements that make up the visual identity
- Visualisation diagram
- Assets table

TASK 2 OVERVIEW

In Task 2, you will use graphics editing software to create the visual identity, create and/or source assets, create the digital graphic products and export them in appropriate file formats and settings.

1 Create the visual identity

Here, you are creating any parts that make up the visual identity, such as the logo, slogan and colour scheme. It is your choice what software you use to make these.

Visual identity assets are used in the final graphical products

2 Create and/or source assets

Now you need to find or create the different assets that you need. Remember to record them in your asset table.

Assets are prepared and saved

3 Prepare and save the assets

You now need to prepare the assets for use in the final graphic. This may require cropping or isolating parts of the image. The resolution should be correct for use in the final image.

Assets are used in the final products

4 Create the digital graphic products

You now need to make the digital products that you have been asked to make in the client brief. In this example, a poster was requested along with a suitable adaptation for use in a web advert.

Poster

Web ad

Final products are exported

5 Export your digital graphic products

It doesn't take long to export your products, so make sure you get all the settings correct for how they will be used. These will need to match any settings and dimensions that you have been given in the client brief.

Print

Barton_Poster.pdf

Settings:
300 DPI
Dimensions: 29.7cm x 21.0 cm
Colour mode: CMYK

Web

Barton_web_advert.png

Settings:
72 DPI
Dimensions: 300 px x 300 px
Colour mode: RGB

SETTING UP A NEW DOCUMENT

When creating a new document to meet a client brief, it is important to set up the size and resolution at the start. If you create a document that is the wrong size it will not fully meet the client requirements.

Document size, orientation and resolution

Size can be measured in several ways including millimetres and pixels. Whichever you use, check it meets the client requirements as it is easy to get confused between the different measurement types.

The orientation of the paper means whether it is turned so that it is portrait (height is longer than width) or landscape (width is longer).

Print documents require a resolution of 300 PPI. Make sure this is set for any assets or documents that will be printed. You can always export lower resolutions if you need them for web documents. Web documents may be set to 72 PPI.

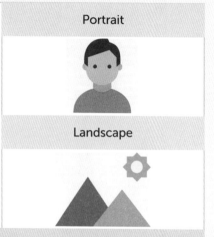

Portrait

Landscape

Example settings for a new document

The created document dimensions

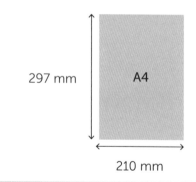

297 mm

A4

210 mm

! Note

- Graphics editing software has many features and requires many hours of practice to be able to use. This section gives you an understanding of the different tools and the effects they have. It is not an instructional how-to guide. Be prepared to search on the Internet to find out how to use tools you aren't familiar with.

- In this section, screenshots and settings are taken from Photoshop. Very similar tools and settings will be present in other graphics editing software such as Affinity® Photo and GIMP.

IMPORTANT!
Remember that before you start building your final graphical product, you need to source and create all the assets needed. See more information about this on **pages 45** & **93**.

Image size

The **image size** may be altered after you have created or opened a file. This changes the size of the whole image, for example, to create a smaller version of a graphic for use on a web image. By default, the image remains in proportion, meaning the width and height will change relative to each other so the image is not distorted.

The resolution can also be changed here, for example to create a lower resolution version of a graphic for use online.

Image size: 200 × 100 px

Image size:
100 × 50 px

Canvas size

This changes the size of the **canvas** or page that the image sits on rather than the image. When the canvas is made larger, it will create space around the original image.

If the canvas is made smaller than the image, it will crop some of the image. It is best to use the correct canvas size before you begin editing.

Here the canvas size has been increased by 50 px on each side. The checked grey and white grid shows the new canvas area which is currently transparent.

- Check carefully that the document size and resolution meet the client requirements.
- If a resolution isn't given, select a suitable one for the graphical product you are creating.
- If you are asked to make a product for print and web, first make the image at a resolution of 300 DPI. You can decrease the image size or resolution at a later stage.

LAYOUT TOOLS

Before placing objects onto the canvas, it is a good idea to make use of **grids**, **guides** and **rulers**.

Rulers, guides and grids

Depending on the software you use, you may need to turn on the viewing of rulers and gridlines. In Photoshop, this is found on the View menu.

Rulers display a ruler above and to the left of the image. They are useful for giving a idea of measurements on the screen. **Grids** help when visually lining up objects and checking the spacing between them. The graphics editing software may also try to snap objects to the grid.

Guides are very useful when trying to align images or text. You should be able to set up guides to an exact position in pixels. It is easier to drag guides where you want them. To do this in Photoshop, first make sure the ruler is being shown. Then click and hold in the ruler bar which enables you to drag the guideline into the image. Use the horizontal and vertical rulers to create horizontal and vertical guides.

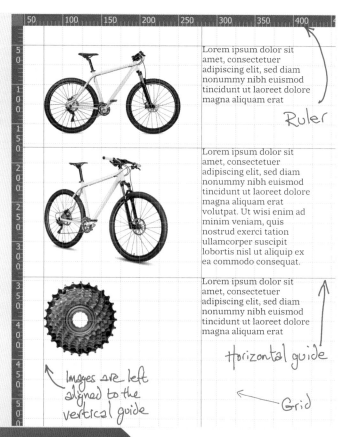

Ruler

Horizontal guide

Grid

Images are left aligned to the vertical guide

In Photoshop, double clicking the ruler will bring up preferences. Here you are able to change the ruler units to be pixels, centimetres or millimetres.

In Photoshop, the shortcut to show and hide the grid is CTRL+ ' (Windows) or CMD + ' (Mac). The ' symbol is the key next to the # symbol.

DRAWING TOOLS

Shapes

Image editing packages include a range of shape **drawing tools** to enable you to add rectangles, ellipses, triangles, polygons, lines, and custom shapes to your graphic.

Rectangle

Rectangle with curved edges

Polygon

Triangle

Rectangle Tool	U
Ellipse Tool	U
Triangle Tool	U
Polygon Tool	U
Line Tool	U
Custom Shape Tool	U

Think carefully about how shapes may be used to enhance your graphic in subtle ways. For instance, a triangle may be rotated to create a bullet point; a line may be used to separate sections of text.

This is the first bullet point

This is the second bullet point

Many icons in the menu may have sub-menus. Depending on your software, you may need to hover or click and hold to see the sub-menu.

Shapes may even be used to make icons. These would be made as new documents and exported as individual assets to put in your final digital graphic.

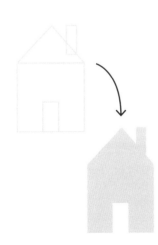

Fills and strokes

Shapes can be filled with colour – this is known as the **fill** colour. The fill may be a solid colour, a gradient fill or a transparent colour (which means there won't be any fill colour).

The line around a shape is known as a **stroke**. The thickness of the stroke may be changed. The style may also be altered to create a dashed line.

Colour selection

When altering colours, open the **colour picker**. You may need to double click the colour you want to change on the toolbar to open it. Fills and strokes may have different colours or be transparent.

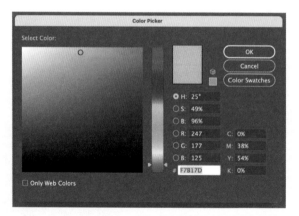

Remember, that you should have already created a colour scheme as part of your visual identity. Ideally, you should have also recorded the RGB values or hex colour codes. If so, enter this in the appropriate boxes so that you get a perfect match with your colour scheme.

Gradients

A **gradient** is a gradual blend from one colour to another. Different options are available such as linear (in a straight line) or radial (circular).

A linear gradient from purple to white inside a rectangle shape.

Here a linear gradient fades from purple to violet. The opacity (transparency) of the violet has also been changed to zero making the box fade out and revealing the background.

Gradients often improve the look of buttons and key areas of a graphic document.

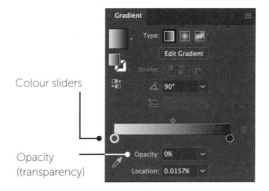

Colour sliders

Opacity (transparency)

IMAGE ADJUSTMENTS

When adding images to your graphic product, you should carefully consider whether any adjustments are required. All the images should work well together and fit with your colour scheme and style. The following image adjustment settings are available to help you achieve this.

Brightness and contrast

Altering the **brightness** and **contrast** will affect the **tonal range** (range of colours) shown in the image.

Original image

Brightness +50

Brightness −50

Original image

Contrast +50

Contrast −50

Colour balance

The **colour balance** allows you to match the colours used in other images to help give a more effective and professional feel.

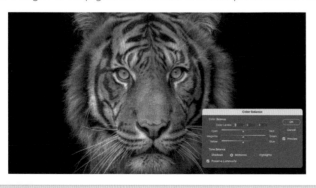

Duplicate the layer before making any significant changes. This way, you'll be able to go back to the original layer if you make a mistake.

Hue and saturation

Hue

Hue is the underlying base colour of an image. Altering the hue allows you to alter an image's colour. This is a useful tool in helping to match an image with your colour scheme. It is also useful in creating background images. In Photoshop, the Colorize option will make any alterations to Hue apply to the whole image.

Saturation

Saturation is how intense or rich colours are in the image. Increasing the saturation will make your image more vibrant and engaging.

Original image

Saturation +50

Hue 360 with Colorize selected

Levels

Levels are a more advanced tool that allows both the tonal range and colour balance to be altered all in one place. This is an advanced tool which needs practice and consideration before using correctly.

Original image

Edited image

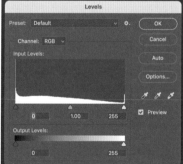

It is tempting when discovering image adjustments for the first time to use extreme alterations. Remember that you are trying to enhance your images so that they match the colour scheme and overall style that you were going for.

SELECTION TOOLS

Selection tools allow you to select parts of an image. Once a selection is made, part of an image may be copied to a new layer or new image. Selection tools are very useful in isolating an object from the background. This may then be saved as an asset for your final graphical product. Alternatively, it may be pasted to a new layer.

There are different ways to make selections based on the type of object you want to select. Some of the selection tools given below may appear on sub-menus of other tools.

Rectangular Marquee tool

The **rectangular marquee selection tool** allows a rectangle or square to be selected. This allows part of an image to be selected. You may then copy this and paste to a new layer or file. This is useful when creating assets.

Elliptical Marquee tool

The **elliptical marquee tool** allows circles and ovals to be selected. You may need to hold down the SHIFT key to make the selection a circle. The selected image is now pasted to a new layer, isolating the image from the background.

You are likely to use selections when making assets. Make sure that there is no background layer and that you have a checked background showing on any parts of the image that should be transparent.

To copy a layer, use CTRL-C or CMD-C.
To paste a new layer with your selection, use CTRL-V or CMD-V.
To select the inverse (opposite) of the selection, use CTRL-SHIFT-I.

Polygon lasso tool

The **polygon lasso tool** creates a path around an object by setting anchor points at the corners of the object. The lines created need to join together to make a polygon. This is useful for selecting objects made up of straight lines.

Magnetic lasso tool

The **magnetic lasso tool** works by automatically snapping (moving) to where there is an obvious edge on an object. If an incorrect snap is made, press the DELETE key. To force an alternative point in the selection just click to create one.

Magic wand tool

The **magic wand tool** selects an area that all has the same colour. Often, you will find that the magic wand tool selects the background. Use the select inverse option to select the object.

Make use of the magic wand context menu when making selections.

Add or subtract to the selection

The tolerance is how close the colour needs to be to the selected colour in order to be added to the selection

LAYERS

Your final graphic will be built up using multiple **layers**. Layers stack on each other like a stack of transparent sheets. This allows assets to be placed over a background.

Using layers

When you alter the graphics inside one layer, you don't alter any others. When you are trying out different ideas within one layer, it may be useful to make a duplicate layer and hide it. Then if you make a mistake, simply delete the layer and unhide the duplicated one.

The **Layers window** shows each layer and their order. The layer at the top of the layer stack is on top of the others. You can drag the layers up or down to reorder whether they are above or below other layers. Layers may be locked to prevent them from being moved by mistake.

It is possible to select two or more layers and **merge** them together. This allows all merged graphics to have filters or effects applied as one layer. Alternatively, two or more layers may be **grouped** together. This preserves original layers.

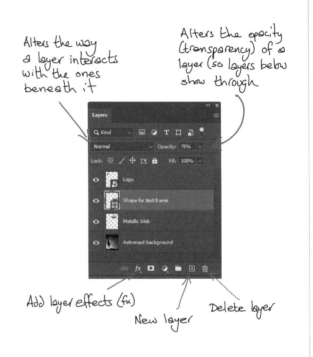

Alters the way a layer interacts with the ones beneath it

Alters the opacity (transparency) of a layer (so layers below show through)

Add layer effects (fx)

New layer

Delete layer

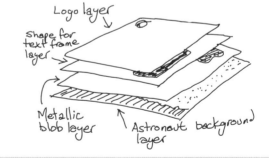

Logo layer

Shape for text frame layer

Metallic blob layer

Astronaut background layer

New layers have names such as Layer 1 or Rectangle 1. Make sure that you change the layer names to something more meaningful. This will help you identify them later. Double clicking the layer name should allow you to change it.

Final layout

Logo

Metallic blob

Astronaut background

shape/frame for text, opacity of 75% allows the background to show through

Layer styles

Different **layer styles**, also known as layer effects, may be applied to each layer in your image. Some examples for the text box shape are shown below.

A drop shadow helps make objects stand out on the page.

The outer glow effect is used here to give the effect of the sun shining on the back of the rectangle.

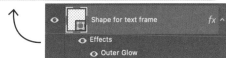

Shape for text frame   fx ^

Effects

Outer Glow

Bevel and emboss has been used here to make the shape appear more like the blob above it.

RETOUCHING

Retouching images allows you to make improvements and finishing touches to images.

Healing brush

The **healing brush** performs a similar function as the spot healing brush, however, you first need to select an area of the image to sample. In Photoshop, hold down CTRL to select the sample area. In this example, an area of smooth skin would be sampled and then brushed over a spot.

Healing brush →

Spot healing brush

The **spot healing brush** allows you to brush over parts of an image that are not required or to remove any imperfections. The software will then determine which pixels to replace the section with.

Spot healing brush →

Clone stamp tool

The **clone stamp tool** allows you to take parts of an image and clone them somewhere else. This may be used for small amounts of retouching, or for cloning whole objects as shown here.

Clone stamp tool →

Blur tool

The **blur tool** allows you to brush over an area to make it more blurred. This may be used to make a particular object stand out. It also may make a text area easier to read above the blurred area as shown below.

Blur tool

Colour picker and swatches

Colour pickers allow you to select colours from all available colours. The **eye dropper tool** is useful for selecting the colour of a specific pixel in an image. This may be added to a **swatch** for use later.

Pencil tool and brush tool

The retouching tools in graphics editing software are often very sophisticated. However, they may not be accurate enough. You may still need to use tools such as the **pencil tool** to alter individual pixels or the **brush tool** to paint and erase.

The pencil tool has a hard edge, whilst the brush tool behaves more like a paint brush would.

Pencil tool

Brush tool

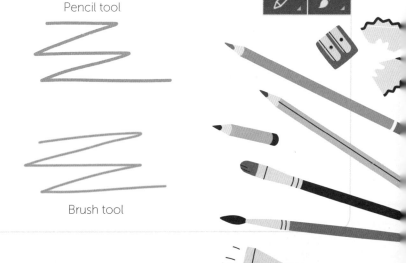

FILTERS AND EFFECTS

There are many **filters and effects** that may be used to enhance or change the visual appeal of an image.

Making images monochrome

There are a number of ways to make an image monochrome. The method used here, creates a new layer and fills it with black using the **paint bucket tool**. The layer blending mode is then set to 'Color'. This is a useful technique to know in the 'colouring images' examples below.

Colouring images

Images may be given a colour wash. This may be used to match with a colour scheme and is also useful in creating background images or backgrounds behind text. The method here has used a layer with an green colour blend. This allows you to easily change the colour.

Having a black and white image with some colour will help draw the eye to a point of interest and creates a striking effect. Simply use the same technique as above to make a layer with a colour blend, then use the eraser tool to remove the fill where you want the colour to appear.

1. Make layer, fill with black and change to 'Colour' blend.

2. Use eraser tool on areas where colour is needed.

! Note

Filters and effects may enhance an image with a dramatic look. However, use them carefully. Applying unnecessary filters or effects may detract from the overall design and lead to a lower quality graphical product.

Colour toning

It is often a good idea to change the colour or tone of an image. This helps to give a different mood to the image or match other images. One way to alter the colour is to use the image adjustments on **pages 104 & 105**. Alternatively, you may choose to use adjustment layers. These allow the settings to be changed in the same way, without altering the original image. If you don't like the result, simply delete the adjustment layer.

Add an adjustment layer – found in the layer menu in Photoshop

Change the levels

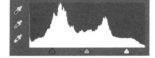

Vignette

A vignette fades a photo into the background. To create a vignette in Photoshop, add a new fill layer choosing a gradient fill.

Add new gradient fill layer

Sharpen

The sharpen filter increases the contrast at edges in a photo to make it appear sharper. This may improve an image, but be aware that it cannot bring an out of focus image into focus.

TYPOGRAPHY

Typography covers the appearance of text. In graphics editing software you have far more control over your text than a typical word processor. Effects, such as drop shadows and gradient fills, may be applied to the text by applying effects to the text layer.

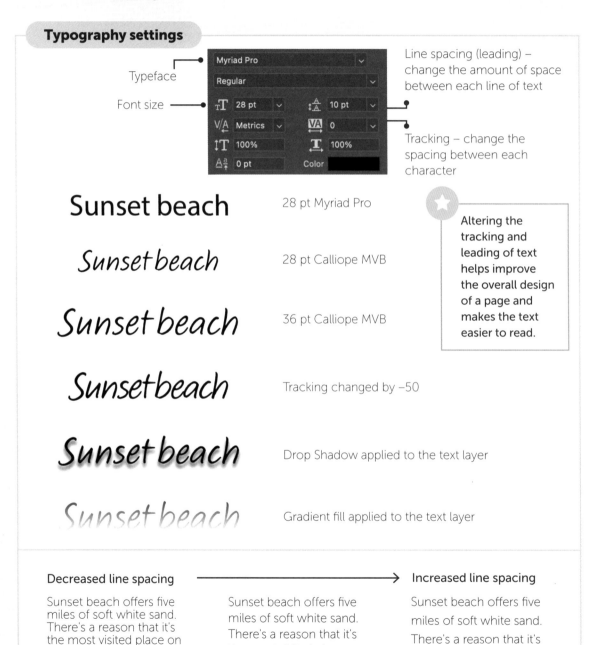

Typography settings

Typeface

Font size

Line spacing (leading) – change the amount of space between each line of text

Tracking – change the spacing between each character

Sunset beach — 28 pt Myriad Pro

Sunset beach — 28 pt Calliope MVB

Sunset beach — 36 pt Calliope MVB

Sunsetbeach — Tracking changed by −50

Sunset beach — Drop Shadow applied to the text layer

Sunset beach — Gradient fill applied to the text layer

> Altering the tracking and leading of text helps improve the overall design of a page and makes the text easier to read.

Decreased line spacing ——————————→ Increased line spacing

Sunset beach offers five miles of soft white sand. There's a reason that it's the most visited place on the island.

Sunset beach offers five miles of soft white sand. There's a reason that it's the most visited place on the island.

Sunset beach offers five miles of soft white sand. There's a reason that it's the most visited place on the island.

SOURCING ASSETS

When creating a digital graphic, you will need to **source**, or find, suitable assets to use. This might include photographs, icons and other graphics.

Sources

There are three main sources of images that you are likely to use:

Internet

You can use a search engine to find suitable images by using a keyword search and filters to narrow your options.

Image libraries

There are many stock libraries that exist, however, for your assessment you are not expected to pay for images. Instead, you may like to use one of the sites offering Creative Commons images such as **Pixabay**, **Pexels** or **Unsplash**.

Client libraries

If the client has provided any images for use, for example a logo, this should be used within the digital graphic.

Using a search engine

A search engine allows you to find images from all over the Internet but can sometimes return many results. To narrow down the choices, you can filter the search results to make the images you see more relevant to your needs.

By selecting **Tools** you can filter the search results by their size, main colours, document types, time created and whether or not they are licensed under Creative Commons licence.

For the NEA, you do not need to obtain any licences or request permission to use images – but you must state in your asset table what you would need to do to use the image in a commercial product.

More information about sourcing assets and searching for images may be found on **pages 92** & **93**.

Downloading assets

When downloading assets from the Internet, they will often be saved into a downloads folder by default. It is important that assets are copied into an appropriate folder before using them.

For example, within your assignment folder structure, it would be helpful to have a folder for both original and edited assets as shown.

It is also important to rename assets with appropriate names. This makes them easier to identify later.

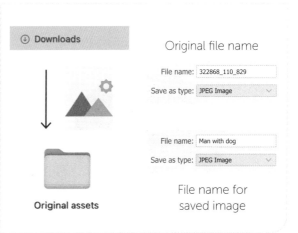

Original file name

File name: 322868_110_829
Save as type: JPEG Image

File name: Man with dog
Save as type: JPEG Image

Original assets

File name for saved image

CREATING ASSETS

When creating your graphics product, you will need to create assets as well as sourcing them online. This could include:

- **Editing an asset** you have sourced to create a new one (known as a **derivative asset**).
- **Creating a new asset** using drawing tools in image editing software.

Editing an existing asset

There are various tools available in image editing software to allow to you edit an existing asset. Some examples of where you might edit an existing asset to make a derivative one include:

- Removing the background of an image
- Adjusting the brightness and contrast
- Making a colour adjustment
- Cropping or rotating an asset
- Using filters

 Provide evidence of your edits to make clear the changes you have made. To do this, take screenshots and annotate them.

Software types

Both bitmap and vector image editing software may be used to create original assets.

You are expected to use bitmap graphic editing software, so in general you should choose this. However, logos in particular, often are best designed in software such as Illustrator, Affinity® Designer or Inkscape. Once a logo has been created it may be exported in an SVG or EPS format.

Drawing tools can be used to draw simple shapes or be combined to create more complex graphics. There are a variety of standard shapes available within image editing software. In addition, the **Direct Selection tool** can be used to alter points of a shape to make irregular ones.

This bitmap logo is a derivative asset that has been created. The oak tree was sourced from an image library. The background was removed, and text added before saving as a PNG file to preserve the transparency.

This vector logo was created in vector graphic software. It was exported and saved as an SVG file for use in the final image.

LUCAS SCOTT

Example client brief

Lucas Scott is a singer that has just completed his latest solo album called 'Fragment'. An album CD cover is needed that will show the artist starting to disintegrate in an eye-catching way.

Example

For this project, a visual identity was first created. A blue colour scheme was chosen and the mood board showed fragmented images. The visualisation diagram shows Lucas Scott in the centre of the CD cover with annotation showing a disintegration effect. Assets now need to be sourced. One asset that is to be created is the image of Lucas Scott.

First, a photograph of Lucas from a photo shoot has been provided to be used on the CD cover.

Asset	Properties	Source	Legal issues	Use
Lucas59.jpg	3648 x 2736 300DPI	Original image from photographer	Signed model release form	CD cover, main image

Now an asset has been made for use in the final graphic. Lots of graphics editing techniques have been used to create this image asset, so a commentary and evidence have also been provided. Once saved, this asset will also need to be added to the asset table.

Development of the main image

To make the main cover photo asset, I first duplicated the photo so that there was a duplicate layer. I then selected the white background using the magic wand tool and removed it.

Next, I applied a Wind 'stylize' filter with a blast effect to give the effect of the face being fragmented.

I then added another layer which I changed to a colour blend mode. I applied a blue colour from the colour scheme in my visual identity.

Finally, I used the eraser tool on the left of the image to show the original face from the lower layer on the left, and the 'wind' filtered face on the right.

TECHNICAL COMPATIBILITY

When sourcing images to use as assets, it is important to check their technical compatibility to ensure they are suitable for use within print graphics.

It is always best to try and source an image or graphic that is an appropriate size and resolution (DPI), however it is possible to change these properties once you have the image.

Resizing and resampling

Resizing and **resampling** makes an image larger or smaller to suit a purpose. Both the pixel dimensions and the dpi can be edited within image editing software by entering new measurements.

When creating print products, make sure all your assets have a resolution of 300 DPI.

If you untick the 'resample' box, the image width and height will change to reflect the new resolution. If you want to keep the image dimensions the same, tick 'resample' and the software will calculate any missing pixels. This works well when reducing the resolution, but be careful when increasing the resolution or image dimensions as quality will be lost.

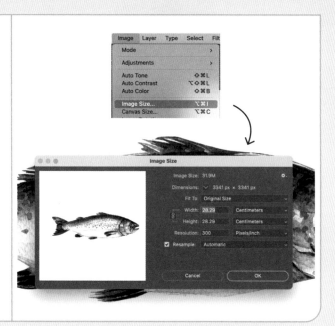

Rasterising vector graphics

Vectors make use of lines, fills and curves to create shapes and illustrations. Sometimes when using graphics editing software, in order to use certain features you may need to convert vector layers to bitmaps. This is especially true in older versions of software.

In general, if possible, try to keep graphics and text in their vector format. This will make sure your graphic has the highest quality when you carry out your final export.

If a graphics editing feature needs the asset or layer to be rasterised, then of course, do this. Be aware that you will lose the ability to edit the vector.

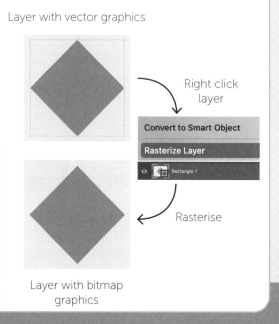

Layer with vector graphics

Right click layer

Convert to Smart Object

Rasterize Layer

Rasterise

Layer with bitmap graphics

Storing assets for use

When choosing a **storage location** to store your assets you need to clearly differentiate between the original and the edited assets by using separate folders.

It is also important to consider the **file format** used for your assets. For instance, you may need to save as a PNG file with transparency for a logo asset.

Equally, you will probably want to save any original editing files such as a Photoshop .psd file. This stores all the layers, vectors and settings that were used when creating the graphic. This will allow you to go back and change assets if they don't look right once they are imported into your final graphic.

Name		Kind
> 📁 Original assets		Folder
> 📁 Edited assets		Folder

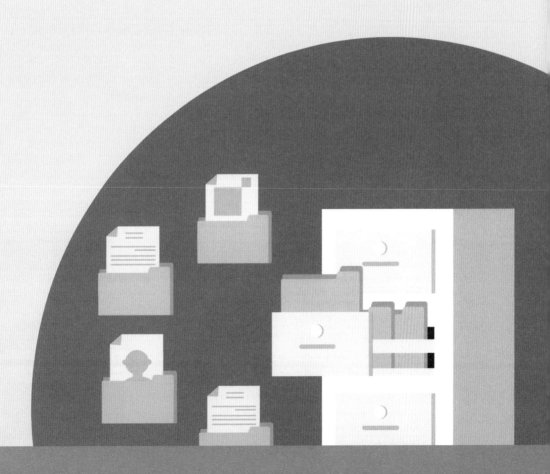

DOM HALL SNOWBOARDING

Example client brief

Dom Hall is a snowboarding instructor in Chamonix, France. He runs a snowboarding school teaching snowboarding to teenagers and young adults. He has just made his first DVD for a series of DVDs which will be called 'Learn to snowboard'.

Dom Hall needs a visual identity for use in the series. He then needs a DVD cover for the first DVD which will be for beginners. The brand should feel dynamic and engaging to help complement Dom's style of teaching.

You need to make:

- A visual identity
- A DVD cover as a single digital graphic which includes front, back and spine. The dimensions will be:
    - Front/back cover 130 mm (width) x 184 mm (height) with a spine of 8 mm
    - An online version of the front cover only, cropped or resized to a width of 800 pixels.

Example

Once you have created your assets for your visual identity and the product, you need to show that they have been saved using the correct settings.

Assets

I found the background mountains image and recorded it in my assets table.

Before I started any editing, I changed the resolution of the image to 300 DPI so that it would be suitable for the printed DVD cover.

I then added the text. The background of the logo was white which wasn't suitable as an asset for the final graphic. I used the magic want to select the white background and removed it.

I saved the asset in PSD format in case I needed to make any edits later. I also exported it as a PNG file so that the transparency would be preserved when I add it to the final graphic.

The logo files are stored in my edited assets folder.

Name	Type	Size
Logo	PNG File	39 KB
Logo	Adobe Photoshop...	122 KB

The original mountains image that I sourced for the background is stored in the original assets folder.

Name	Type
Edited assets	File Folder
Original assets	File Folder

Remember that you need to show evidence of the tools that you used when developing the graphic. This is especially important when they are not obvious.

Snowboarder asset

The project brief wanted a dynamic and engaging style. The snowboarder image that I chose showed snow flying behind suggesting speed. I wanted the colours to be even more vibrant in the final image, so I added an adjustment layer to alter the vibrance and saturation of the image.

I saved the snowboarder asset as a JPG as it doesn't need any transparency. I made sure to use a good quality of compression so that no noticeable digital artefacts were present. Both a PSD editing file and JPG exported file were created.

It is much easier to record evidence of actions you take as you go along. Each lesson, when you are editing images, take a few screenshots of key techniques you have carried out and save them into a folder or directly in your report. This will make sure that you have evidence at the end of the assessment.

File formats such as Photoshop PSD or Affinity® Photo AFPHOTO are only suitable for use when editing. They are proprietary formats that are used for master files that are able to be edited.

All the assets that you need for the final digital graphic should all be located in two folders. One for the original assets and one for the edited assets. It is important that you save files in appropriate formats.

For instance, if using Photoshop, any editing files will be stored in PSD format. Assets that require transparency will be **exported** to PNG format, whilst photos may be exported to JPG or PNG format. Vector graphics will need to be saved or exported in SVG or EPS format.

You don't need to record evidence of obvious edits you made such as adding an image. If though, you made image adjustments, such as altering the colours, or removing the background, these should be evidenced in your report.

Asset folders

 Original assets

Name	Type ^	Size
Dom Hall - front cover main image	JPG File	131 KB
Instructing snowboarders	JPG File	104 KB
Jump	JPG File	18 KB
Logo - mountains	JPG File	21 KB
Snowboarders	JPG File	19 KB
Stop	JPG File	19 KB
Exemption	PNG File	43 KB

 Edited assets

Name	Type ^	Size
Barcode	Adobe Photoshop...	94 KB
Dom Hall - front cover main image	Adobe Photoshop...	8,632 KB
Exemption	Adobe Photoshop...	277 KB
Instructing snowboarders	Adobe Photoshop...	5,522 KB
Jump	Adobe Photoshop...	744 KB
Logo	Adobe Photoshop...	122 KB
Snowboarders	Adobe Photoshop...	918 KB
Stop	Adobe Photoshop...	840 KB
Dom Hall - front cover main image	JPG File	131 KB
Instructing snowboarders	JPG File	104 KB
Jump	JPG File	18 KB
Snowboarders	JPG File	19 KB

When developing both assets and your final product, be sure to look carefully at your work and consider any improvements you can make. Your image needs to be effective to gain higher marks.

Now carry out the following:
- Make folders to store your original and edited assets.
- Source all your assets.
- Create and edit the assets as required.
- Update your assets table.
- Save assets in the appropriate location and format.
- Evidence any tools or editing that you carried out when creating the assets.

THE FINAL DIGITAL PRODUCT

Once all your assets are created, you are able to build your final digital product.

Saving master files

As you develop your final product you need to make sure that you save your master files so that you are able to make any changes to them if needed.

These will be saved in a proprietary format such as PSD or AFPHOTO.

For print graphics, in Photoshop, simply use the 'Save As...' option and change the filetype.

Saving versions

Remember to save versions of your final product as you create it. If you make a mistake, you will always be able to go back to a previous version.

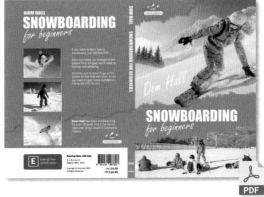

- Give evidence of the tools and techniques you used by adding screenshots and annotation to your report.
- Make sure to check the dimensions and resolution of your final image match those given in the client brief before saving.

See pages 101 to 114 for tools and techniques which will help you to build your digital product.

REPURPOSING

The main graphic created for this project was the DVD cover. The client brief also asks for an online version to be created with a width of 800 pixels.

In this case, the **repurposing** of the graphic is simply a case of cropping the DVD cover then exporting using an appropriate file format.

When cropping the image, make sure that it is the exact dimensions requested in the client brief.

Export as PNG

W : 130.0 mm
H : 184.0 mm

Front cover for online use
Format: PNG
Resolution 72 PPI
Colour space RGB
Dimensions 130 × 184 mm

Before saving your repurposed image, make sure that the image size and resolution are correct. See **pages 98**, **99** & **118** for more details.

SAVING AND EXPORTING

File formats

When **saving and exporting** there are several different file formats you are able to choose from. Some of these are more appropriate for print, whilst others are more appropriate for use on a website/multimedia. Key file formats that you are likely to use are shown below.

File format	Print	Web or multimedia
PDF	Yes – this is a good choice for print products.	Not for using as part of a web page. Only suitable for products that show within a dedicated PDF viewer – such as a brochure, report or book.
PNG	No.	Yes – this preserves transparency.
JPG	Yes – but not a good choice if it contains text.	Yes – but it doesn't have transparency and doesn't work well with text.
TIFF	Yes - suitable for high quality images.	No.

Professional printing companies typically will accept PDFs for print products such as book covers and posters.

In Photoshop, you are able to save your image as a PDF in the Save As... option.

If the image editing software you are using doesn't allow you to save as a PDF, then for the purpose of the assessment, exporting or saving a high resolutions JPG image will be acceptable if you've been asked to produce a print product.

Dimensions, resolution and colour space

When creating print files, you should use 300 DPI and the CMYK colour space. If you need to re-purpose a print file for use in websites or multimedia products, first save a copy. You can now change the resolution to 72 PPI. You can also change the colour space to RGB.

	Print	Web or multimedia
Resolution	300 DPI	72 DPI
Dimensions	These are typically given in millimetres or centimetres. Make sure you match any dimensions given in the client brief.	These are typically given in pixels. Make sure you match any pixel dimensions given in the client brief.
Colour space	CMYK	RGB

Now carry out the following:

- Create your digital graphic product.
- Save the product in a suitable file format.
- Repurpose the product for a different use.
- Export the new graphic product into an appropriate file format.
- Add appropriate evidence to your report of tools used and file settings chosen.

Creating the visual identity and digital graphic product

In Task 2 you will be asked to create the visual identity and other assets needed for your final product. You will also need to repurpose your final product for another use and export it. Use these pages to make sure you have completed everything you need to do for Task 2.

Remember that the assets you need to make will depend on what you have added to your visualisation diagram. Remember to use suitable file formats and settings for the final products that you save or export.

Stage	Task	Completed
Create folders	Create folders to store your original assets, edited assets and final graphical products.	☐
Create the visual identity and other assets	Create each of the elements that make up the visual identity. Save the elements of the visual identity.	☐
	Create/source the other assets for your digital graphic product. Prepare and save the assets.	☐
	Give explicit evidence showing all assets have the correct file format, correct dimensions and correct resolution.	☐
Create the digital graphic products	Create your digital graphic product with image editing software.	☐
	Repurpose the digital graphic for another use.	☐
	Check that your digital graphic products match the requirements given in the client brief.	☐
Export the digital graphic products	Save/Export the digital graphic products with the: • Correct file formats • Correct dimensions • Correct resolution (DPI / PPI)	☐
Report	Add evidence of how you have used and applied the concepts of graphic design and layout conventions in your work.	☐
	Show how your digital graphics were made including annotated screenshots of the tools that were used.	☐

Evidence you should have in files or your report:

- Evidence of concepts of graphic design.
- Evidence of the tools and techniques you used in image editing software, including screenshots.
- Visual identity assets including the logo in electronic format.
- The final graphic products in electronic format.

EXAMINATION PRACTICE ANSWERS

(a)   Radio [1], print publishing [1], interactive media [1], internet [1], digital publishing [1]. Film and television
       are not appropriate sectors here as FastFit don't want any video. Computer games are unlikely to be appropriate for
       promoting a local sports centre.   [2]

(b)   Radio advertisement [1], social media graphic/post [1], leaflet [1], poster [1], billboard [1], podcast [1] or other
       suitable product. [1]   [3]

(c)   A campaign manager would be responsible for overseeing the whole campaign [1] including how it works in conjunction
       with the website [1] and making sure everyone in the team meets their deadlines [1]. The campaign manager will set objectives
       for the director to meet [1]. By contrast, a camera operator is one team member/crew [1] who works under the director [1]
       and is responsible for framing shots to achieve the emotion and messages that need to be captured in the video. [1]   [4]

(d)   Copy writer [1], script writer [1], sound editor [1], audio technician [1], creative director [1], director [1],
       production manager [1]. Accept other appropriate roles.   [2]

(e)   C. Pre-production.   [1]

(f)   A video editor will select the most appropriate shots and scenes [1] that capture the mood and vision of the director/
       campaign manager [1]. They will combine components such as sound that has been recorded by an audio technician [1]
       and video footage from the camera operator [1]. They will make sure that all clips fit into the 30 second target time[1].
       They will trim clips [1] so that only the best content is used / poor footage is rejected. [1]   [3]

(g)   Web designer [1], web developer [1], graphic designer [1], photographer [1], copy writer. [1]   [3]

(h)   They could add the video to a post [1] which they share on a social media platform [1]. They could write a blog post /
       article [1] that includes the video [1] highlighting key features of the new gym [1]. Accept other examples of how the video
       could be shared on the Internet, websites or social media.   [4]

(i)   Production manager.   [1]

(a)   To promote [1] the book and make the reader want to pick it up and read it, [1] to inform [1] the reader about the title,
       author and content [1].   [2]

(b)   Gender [1], location[1], interests[1], lifestyle[1], ethnicity/religion/culture[1]. Note that income level and occupation
       are ways to segment audiences, however, they would not be appropriate methods for a audience of young children.   [2]

(c)   The colour scheme chosen could be dark and mysterious [1] helping the audience understand that a mystery will
       develop. [1] Characters could be shown from a scene in the book [1] so that the audience is able to imagine themselves
       in the scenario. [1] The graphics would make use of either detailed illustration or photographs[1] as these would be more
       appealing to the age group[1]. Accept other descriptions that are appropriate for the target age group.   [2]

(d)   Focus group [1], questionnaire [1], online survey[1], interview [1].   [1]

(e)   Focus groups: A set of ideas could be shown [1] to a group from the target audience. [1]. They then could give feedback in a
       discussion. [1]. Ideas that are very similar could be shown [1] so that the group is able to feedback on which one they prefer [1].
       Questionnaire/survey: People who form the target audience [1] could be shown the book cover and asked a series of
       questions about it [1] via a form. [1]
       Interview: People who form the target audience [1] could be shown the book cover and asked about their views [1] then
       asked follow-up questions. [1]   [3]

(f)   By referring to the results from the market research, the graphic designer will understand what appeals to the reader [1] and
       what design styles are less effective. [1] It will give them ideas that will stand out from other books in the genre [1] and help to
       tempt readers to choose the book[1]. Accept other reasonable design decisions that could be based on market research.   [2]

(g)   A close up of a child's face [1] would show their eyes / mouth / face [1] allowing the viewer to see happiness / pleasure. [1]
       A mid shot of the child reading the book under a duvet lit by a torch [1] would help to suggest that they can't wait to find out
       what happens. [1]
       Accept other shot types with a suitable explanation.   [2]

(h) Drop down menu [1], button [1], hotspot [1], rollover button [1], media player [1], form controls / text box / radio buttons / checkboxes[1]. [2]

(i) Colour:
The colours used in the image use dark blues, moonlight and mist [1] which help to darken the mood / suggest mystery. [1]
White text has been used [1] that contrasts with the background / makes the text legible. [1]
Positioning:
The author's name is located at the top [1] which helps loyal fans recognise this as a book they will enjoy. [1]
The positioning/crop of the ship on the page [1] helps to promote the book as pirate fiction. [1]
The slogan is at the bottom of the page to help encourage a potential customer to buy the book. [1] It also helps to suggest the genre of the book as fiction [1] (rather than a historical book). [4]

R093 Exam   Section 3

(a) A - Task [1], B - Milestone[1], C – Activity/subtask. [1]   [3]

(b) If the graphic designer is working in a team, a work plan shows who is responsible for each task [1] so everyone on the team is clear on what tasks/activities they need to do [1]. The graphic designer would be able to see if they are ahead of or behind schedule. [1] They will know when the project is due for completion [1] so be able to determine when they can start another project. [1] Accept other ways in which the workplan could be used.   [3]

(c) Any photos taken with people in would need a model release form [1] to show that they have given their permission to be used on the cover [1]. Any information stored about models / cyclists would need to be stored in line with data protection legislation. [1] For instance, they would need to be stored securely. [1] Any stock photography or images would need to have appropriate licences/permission [1] to use it with appropriate fees paid. [1] Accept other explanations of a legal consideration that is appropriate to this scenario.   [4]

(d) The symbols in order are: trademark, registered trademark, Creative Commons.   [3]

(e) A. Sub node [1], B. Branch/connector. [1]   [2]

(f) To quickly [1] generate ideas for the magazine [1], to show how different ideas for the magazine [1] are connected together [1], to share initial ideas [1] with other members of the team. [1]   [2]

(g) Images/graphics [1], photographs [1], examples of text showing font style/typography [1], colour scheme/colour swatch [1], annotations [1] photos of textures. [1] Do not accept video or music in this case. Although these can be included in a digital mood board, they are not appropriate for a print product.   [2]

(h) Client [1], design team / graphic designer / illustrator / photographer.   [1]

(i) The ASA would be responsible for any of the adverts used in the magazine.   [1]

(j) The personal data will need to be stored securely / encrypted [1] to prevent/reduce the chance of hackers using it / to prevent the chance of ID theft. [1]
The web page will need a link to a privacy policy [1] which will show how the data will be used / processed. [1]
The emails sent will need to have an unsubscribe link [1] so that users are able to remove themselves from the mailing list. [1]
The publishers must allow customers to update their details [1] so that they can change email address. [1]
Accept other appropriate actions that the publishers would need to take along with an explanation.   [2]

(k) Flow chart.   [1]

(l) An example improved draft version is on the following page: [9]
When marking this question, the examiners will be looking for:
- Clarity of the idea.
- Relevance of content (format, styles, suitability).
- Components of visualisation diagram use, including: images, shapes, colours/colour scheme (using annotations/ hatching/shading), font styles, font sizes, positioning/layout information, text (slogan/branding).
- Justifications for improvements (this can be through annotation or overall appearance) e.g., high impact to help encourage people to buy/read, appearance of the magazine cover, use of house style features such as logo, use of conventions such as barcode, price, date and issue number, consideration of appropriateness for a print product. Remember, you aren't marked on your artistic ability, but you need to be accurate and make drawings with care and attention. If you wish to use a ruler for straight lines you may.

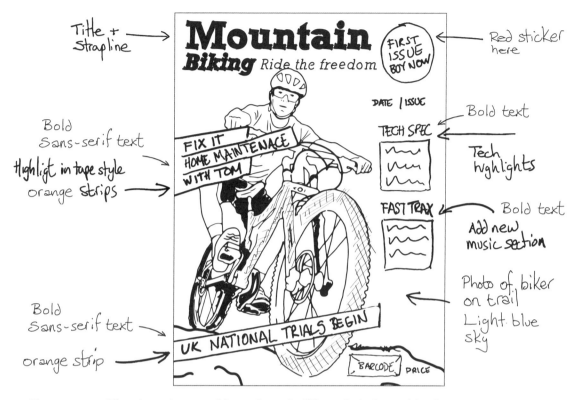

Launch Issue

Title + strapline →

Mountain Biking *Ride the freedom*

FIRST ISSUE BUY NOW

← Red sticker here

DATE / ISSUE

Bold Sans-serif text

Highligt in tape style orange strips

FIX IT HOME MAINTENACE WITH TOM

TECH SPEC ← Bold text

Tech highlights

FAST TRAX ← Bold text

Add new music section

Photo of biker on trail Light blue sky

Bold Sans-serif text →

orange strip →

UK NATIONAL TRIALS BEGIN

BARCODE PRICE

There are many different ways to answer this question so it will be marked using mark bands:

Level 3 (high) 7–9 marks
A **comprehensive** document which shows **detailed** understanding:

- A **range** of suggested improvements are identified.
- Improvements cover a **range** of components.
- Conventions are **effectively** applied.
- Justifications show **detailed** knowledge and **understanding** of the suitability of the document to meet the client's requirements.

Level 2 (mid) 4–6 marks
An **adequate** document which shows **sound** understanding:

- **Some** suggested improvements are identified.
- Improvements cover **some** components.
- Conventions are **adequately** applied.
- Justifications show **sound** knowledge and understanding of the suitability of the document to meet the client's requirements.

Level 1 (low) 1–3 marks
A **basic** document which shows **limited** understanding:

- **Few** suggested improvements are identified.
- Improvements cover **few** components.
- Conventions are applied in a **limited** way.
- Justifications show **limited** knowledge and understanding of the suitability of the document to meet the client's requirements.

0 marks
Response is not worthy of credit.

(m)   An example discussion:

The storyboard has been well drawn which helps to give the video editor a good idea of how the final shots will be ordered and the feeling that the video should give the viewer.

There are currently no transitions mentioned on the storyboard. As the scene is fast paced, I would use cuts for the first two transitions. When transitioning between the wheel swerve and the final text I would use a wipe. I would also pan the camera to follow the mud to the right so that it appears to cover the text. Visual effects could also be added – for instance, the mud spray could fall to reveal the text.

Timings could be added to each frame so that the video editor knows how long the whole video will be and how fast they need to be editing each shot. I would have about 3 seconds on the first frame with slow motion. This would give suspense to what is about to come. I would then have normal speed for panels two and three with each lasting just one second. The faster pace will help to add excitement and energy.

Finally, I would animate the SIGN UP NOW text with an arrow appearing next to it. This would be able to indicate where the viewer is to sign up on the web page and help increase the number of people who sign up to the mailing list.

When marking this question, you need to show your improvements and explanations of how these make the storyboard more effective. The examiners will be looking for:

- Location details within the panels.
- Showing transitions such as cut, dissolve, wipe
- Giving panels scene numbers and/or shot numbers
- Showing timings
- Showing any effects/special effects/visual effects that need to be added
- Suggesting a different order to panels
- Making descriptions/annotation clearer
- Ensuring the content in the panels is consistent
- Explaining the suitability for the target audience. Remember that in this case the audience is the video editor.
- Making use of media terminology related to storyboards and adverts

Level 3 (high) 7–9 marks

A **thorough** discussion which shows **detailed** understanding:

- A **range** of strengths and weaknesses are identified.
- Discussion shows **detailed** knowledge and understanding of the suitability of the storyboard for the video editor
- A **range** of suggested improvements are identified
- How the effectiveness is improved is **clearly** explained
- **Consistently** uses appropriate terminology

Level 2 (mid) 4–6 marks

An **adequate** discussion which shows **sound** understanding:

- **Some** strengths **and/or** weaknesses are identified.
- Discussion shows **sound** knowledge and understanding of the suitability of the storyboard for the video editor or other users/consumers
- **Some** suggested improvements are identified
- How effectiveness is improved is **adequately** explained
- **Sometimes** uses appropriate terminology

Level 1 (low) 1–3 marks

A **brief** discussion which shows **limited** understanding:

- **Few** strengths **or** weaknesses are identified
- Discussion shows **limited** knowledge and understanding of the suitability for consumers/users
- **Few** suggested improvements are identified
- Where improvements to effectiveness are explained, this is done in a **limited** way
- Use of appropriate terminology is **limited**

0 marks

Response is not worthy of credit.

(a)   Resolution is the number of pixels in an image [1]. The higher the resolution, the more accurate / clearer the image is. [1]   [2]

(b)   A suitable dpi for the printed flyer would be **300** dpi. [1] A suitable dpi for the online flyer would be **72** dpi. [1]   [2]

(c)   PDF [1], TIFF [1].   [1]

(d)   SVG.   [1]

(e)   MP4.   [1]

(f)   Exporting means saving the file as a different format [1] that is suitable for viewing in standard media players. [1]   [2]

(g)   2 frames per second means that the frames will change every half a second [1]. This will make movement very jerky [1] and the video will look unprofessional [1].   [2]

(h)   The sample rate is the number of times per second that a sample is taken [1]. It is measured in Hertz (Hz) / kilohertz (kHz) which means 1000 Hz [1]. In this case, 192000 samples of the sound wave are taken each second. [1]   [2]

(i)   Lossy compression will lose some sound quality in the compression process [1]. If the recording company uses a lossy file format, small imperfections will be saved which will reduce the sound quality [1]. These cannot be later restored [1].   {2]

NOTES, DOODLES AND EXAM DATES

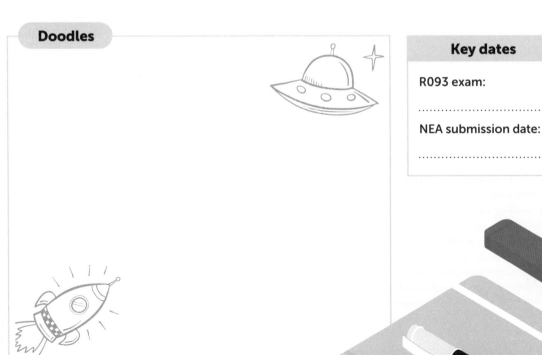

Doodles

Key dates

R093 exam:

....

NEA submission date:

....

SKETCHES AND IDEAS

INDEX

EXAMINATION TIPS

With your examination practice, use a boundary approximation for the examined unit using the following table.
Be aware that boundaries are usually a few percentage points either side of this.

Level	Level 2				Level 1		
Grade	Distinction*	Distinction	Merit	Pass	Distinction	Merit	Pass
Code	2*	D2	M2	P2	D1	M1	P1
Boundary	90%	80%	70%	60%	50%	40%	30%

1. In design-based questions, the examiner can only mark what they can see. Make sure you use either black pen or an HB pencil only.

2. Use the space wisely in design tasks and ensure that you take up the whole of the available space for your design. You may use a ruler if you need to draw straight lines.

3. Read the questions carefully. For instance, if a question refers to the advantages of a physical mood board, you won't get any marks for mentioning video and audio.

4. In explain questions, marks are usually given as 1 mark for a point and 1 mark for the explanation. Make sure you expand your answer using connective words such as 'because' or 'so'.

5. Make sure your answers apply to the context you are given. For instance, if you are asked for assets that could be included in a book cover, you wouldn't get a mark for saying 'a BBFC certificate' as this would only fit the context of a DVD or film poster.

6. Always try to refer back to the brief or scenario that has been given. Use the information you have been given in the question and make sure you reference it in your answer.

7. Vague answers won't get marks. For instance, if you were asked to give an item that would be included on a visualisation diagram, 'text' would gain no marks as it is ambiguous. More specific answers would include 'banner text', 'annotation of the text size', 'font style'.

8. If a question has a * beside it, it means that the quality of your written communication will be assessed. In your answer to these questions, you will need to write in full sentences to obtain the higher marks.

9. When creating planning documents, such as a visualisation diagram, you should include annotations unless the question says otherwise. Annotation is used to show points such as fonts, colours, sizes and justification for your choices of layout and content.

10. If you are asked to create a storyboard, to get higher marks you need to include technical details such as scene numbers, camera angles, shot type, camera movement and timings. You should aim to use at least three technical details for each scene number.

11. If you are asked to recommend software, your recommendation should be the type of software used in industry. For instance, if you are asked to recommend software for producing a storyboard, desktop publishing, illustration software and graphics software would all get a mark. Word and PowerPoint would not get a mark.

12. When recommending software, brand names of well-known software products are also acceptable (e.g. Desktop Publishing – Adobe InDesign; Graphics software – Adobe Photoshop; Illustration software – Adobe Illustrator).

Good luck!